Mamie's Children

Three Generations of Prairie Women

Judy Schultz

Red Deer College Press

The Publishers
Red Deer College Press
56 Avenue & 32 Street Box 5005
Red Deer Alberta Canada T4N 5H5

Acknowledgments
Cover photograph courtesy of Judy Schultz.
Other photographs courtesy of Ken Harris.
Cover design by Boldface Technologies.
Text design by Dennis Johnson.
Printed and bound in Canada by Webcom Limited for Red Deer College Press.

Excerpt from "old coyote hunting man" in *Grasslands* © 1990 Thelma Poirier. Coteau Books. Used by permission of the publisher.

Financial support provided by the Alberta Foundation for the Arts, a beneficiary of the Lottery Fund of the Government of Alberta, and by the Canada Council, the Department of Canadian Heritage and Red Deer College.

ALBERTA Lotteries
The Alberta Foundation for the Arts
Alberta COMMUNITY DEVELOPMENT
COMMITTED TO THE DEVELOPMENT OF CULTURE AND THE ARTS

THE CANADA COUNCIL FOR THE ARTS SINCE 1957 | LE CONSEIL DES ARTS DU CANADA DEPUIS 1957

Canadian Cataloguing in Publication Data
Schultz, Judy.
Mamie's children
ISBN 0-88995-167-5
1. Harris, Mamie Elizabeth, 1877 – 1961. 2. Frontier and pioneer life—Saskatchewan. 3. Women pioneers—Saskatchewan—Biography. I. Title.
FC3522.1.H37S38 1997   971.24'02'092   C97-910534-8
F1072.H37S38 1997

5 4 3 2 1

at all, and I remember her short legs gave her no lap to speak of either, so when she tried to rock me I felt that I was in constant danger of sliding off.

But she had wonderful eyes, dark and compelling. And her mouth was lovely, with full, sensuous lips. Although she was only five feet tall, she had shapely legs and slender ankles, and was always a little vain about them.

My grandmother's long hair had once been her pride, and many times while she watched my mother twist my own unruly mop into braids, she would remind us both of her former crowning glory. I used to be able to sit on my hair, *she'd tell us, but in the pre-wedding portrait there was no hope of that. Her beautiful hair had been shorn into a shaggy boy's cut, short back and sides because of a recent bout of fever that nearly killed her, and in such cases the shearing was believed essential to a woman's recovery.* All that great mop of long hair—why, it saps the strength right out of a person, *or so Mamie insisted. In the photo, the front of her remaining hair has been frizzed, likely the result of an optimistic attempt at hairstyling by one of her younger sisters.*

THE FIRST THREE YEARS of Mamie's and Ernest's marriage were a financial and personal struggle. With neither the land nor the weather in those few Iowa seasons being to his taste, my grandfather decided to chase his elusive dreams into another grassland state near another border town, to a place called Cody, Nebraska, where he had acquired a section of homestead land.

Ernest was a born horse trader, as much of a gambler as his Christian principles would allow, and there was more than a touch of gypsy about Mamie. During those early years of wandering, she apparently enjoyed the adventure of moving steadily north and west, settling for a while in one state and then another, but prophetically, always near the border.

She had done the unthinkable for a woman of her day: She'd gone out to work, as a cook on the sprawling Metzger ranch, where two thousand head of cattle roamed the grassland and thirty-five hungry ranch hands pulled up to the table for five meals a day. Depending on the season, she'd feed a few more or a few less—less when they were out on cattle drives, more when everybody was in residence. Her cooking stories were part of my childhood mythology, for she and I both found her tales from a ranch kitchen far more entertaining than Mother Goose: *My, but those boys could tuck away the food. Land sakes, I was never finished—hot cakes and ham for early breakfast, steak and eggs for second breakfast, roast for dinner, cakes for afternoon, roast for supper, cakes before bed.* . . . Between regular meals she baked a daily batch of bread and biscuits, made enough cakes and pies and cookies to stock a small bakery, and washed all the dishes by herself.

For her long hours in the ranch kitchen, where she also was allowed to keep and care for her baby, she received no wages. Through an unspecified arrangement, Ernest's horses and cattle were fed in return for her unpaid labor, while he was paid a small wage for part-time work on the Metzger place. Meanwhile, the section of land he'd homesteaded was not as productive as his dreams demanded.

The Family Album

Mamie's first child, Roly, was born in 1897, when she was barely twenty-one, and again she sat for her portrait, this time en famille, *with her hair looking far more abundant and charmingly wispy. Beside her stands my grandfather, a handsome, solemn-looking man with dark, slightly wavy hair and a mustache, holding their infant son. Mamie is still wearing her pensive look, but her expression seems a touch softer, as though she's lost in thought. (In all the pictures I've ever seen, and a few I've taken myself, she managed never to smile for the camera, not even once.)*

IN 1899 MAMIE HAD A SECOND BABY, a daughter she named Edith, always described to me as a sweet, affectionate child who was as cuddly as a puppy. Mamie loved the baby girl extravagantly, loved the way her hair smelled after her bath, loved hearing her laugh—it was

Mamie (age twenty-one), Ernest (age twenty-four) and infant Roly, December 1897.

as though Edith had been a special gift, a doll-sized version of herself. One night shortly after Edith's third birthday, something went wrong, and when Mamie lifted her out of her bed, her tiny body seemed to be burning up with fever. Family members thought it was typhoid, but the more likely culprit would have been a bacterial meningitis, as there's no record of a typhoid epidemic in the area at that time. If a doctor had been available, which is unlikely, he'd have had nothing to offer but sympathy. For Mamie, the end of that day brought the awful knowledge that her child was almost certainly going to die.

I know her desperate prayers; I've said them myself: *Not my child.*

. . . I'll be a better mother, a better wife, but don't take my child. . . . and so on, pleas and promises, the way women did and still do when there's nothing else to be done.

Mamie was holding Edith when the little body seemed to relax, and she knew that the daughter she loved so much had died in her arms. "And so, well, it was over. Edie was gone. I was mad at God for taking her. . . . I didn't see why He needed Edie right then."

In Saskatchewan, there are no statistics on infant mortality prior to 1920, but between 1921 and 1925 the infant mortality rate was 83.2 infant deaths per 1000 live births under one year of age. One year the rate rose to 92, an increase of nearly 10 percent. It began dropping sharply in the late forties. The death of children was so common at that time that family graveyards were often located on farms or ranches throughout the Great Central Plains.

The loss of a child is at once life's greatest irony and its ultimate sadness. In the natural scheme of things, women expect to see their parents die, and those who marry often outlive their husbands, but it seems a greater and more unnatural hurt that a mother should have to bury her own child. After the baby died Mamie had other children, and she busied herself making a home for Ernest and her family, but she never forgot the daughter she lost.

Mamie told me the story of Edith's death only once, when she was old and somebody I loved had died and I couldn't come to terms with it. And then, as though she had no right to complain and bore no grudge, she said matter of factly, "Lots of women lost children, you know. Almost every family, one way and another. Out there in the country, why, there was lots of little graves. Lots of them."

CHAPTER 3

Ocean of Grass:

1910

It was an ocean of grass, a beautiful green ocean,
rippling and rolling all the way to the horizon.

— ERNEST HARRIS

*I*N 1909 ONE OF ERNEST'S FRIENDS, described to me as "one of the Oakes boys," had been to visit Saskatchewan, a Canadian province bordering North Dakota and Montana. When he came back he could hardly find enough superlatives to lavish on it. It was a latter-day Eden, he said, where the prairie rolled wild and free in every direction. He told of game and good water, and such grass, miles and miles of tall prairie wool, so tall it was past the horse's stirrups.

And land? It was to be had for the asking.

Ernest had probably read the pamphlets published by an army of optimistic Canadian boosters—expansionists, land speculators and government agencies who were in a mad rush to populate Canada's western interior, including the triangle of southern dryland the British explorer, John Palliser, had once declared unfit for human habitation. Ernest and his friend and thousands like them heard the call, and Ernest told Mamie he was going to Canada to check on the possibilities.

It's doubtful there was much discussion of the wisdom of his journey, either of its expense or of what Mamie would do in the interim or what, in fact, would happen if he decided to uproot her once again. It's also doubtful that, given a choice, Mamie or any other woman would willingly leave a home she knew and possibly loved for the danger and uncertainty of a foreign frontier, yet women did it, willy-nilly, in the faithful thousands.

In the clear light of historic hindsight, the party with the most to gain from a population boom in Canada's western interior was not the settlers in their leaky sod shacks, but the Canadian Pacific Railway. The promise of a railway had been the carrot that brought British Columbia into Confederation in 1871, and from that day until the celebrated last spike in 1885, its construction had been a struggle.

An early scandal over the original charter sent Sir John A. Macdonald's conservative government crashing in 1873, but the public's memory is notoriously short, and five years later his promise to complete the much ballyhooed ribbon of steel brought him back. Macdonald's national dream of uniting Canada by rail cost far more than anybody had anticipated, and the project became a bottomless pit of expense, sucking down the money. Right off the top, the tab included $25 million in cash, $37 million in survey costs, plus twenty-five million acres of CPR land and a transportation monopoly to the United States for twenty years. Still, with American expansion pushing ever westward, the Canadian railway was considered essential to uniting this vast, difficult country. Macdonald and his cronies, caucusing over a bottle of port in distant Charlottetown, honestly felt that without it the Canadian West would too soon be absorbed by the United States.

For the CPR, completion was just the first problem. In order to justify its own existence, it had to at least appear to pay its own way, and this could only be done through rapid settlement of the prairies.

Men like Ernest and women like Mamie—they were what the CPR desperately needed.

Although he had a lot of help, it was probably Clifford Sifton, minister of the interior in Wilfred Laurier's administration, who most successfully and unblushingly stretched the truth enough to attract tens of thousands of immigrants to the prairies. The land was so fertile, so productive, and there would be a village every ten miles or at the very least a grain elevator to buy their enormous wheat crops, and the town, with all a town's seductive amenities, would naturally spring up around it. Small wonder settlers saw the prairie homestead as the answer to all their prayers. Between Sifton and the CPR, boosterism acquired a greedy edge, ranging from blatant propaganda to outright lies and occasional fraud, but the newcomers, fueled by hope and possibly a little greed of their own, were only too ready to believe.

If boosterism led Ernest to Saskatchewan, it was discontent with Nebraska that pushed him from behind. The Nebraska farm was too small, the weather had been bad, the crop had been chewed over by grasshoppers. Before Mamie had time to raise a serious objection, Ernest was off to Canada to file for another homestead. Two months later, back he came, glowing with his version of good news.

Mamie, we're moving to Saskatchewan! Start packing!

Well, now. Grassland, eh? Grass was something Mamie understood, and maybe (just *maybe*) this time Ernest would strike pay dirt and settle down. The grassland she knew had always fed America's vast livestock population, all the cattle, and before that the bison, the deer, the elk, and a large though diminishing population of pronghorn antelope. Grass could be trusted.

One of the great anomalies of North America is that while our most important political boundaries run east and west, the natural ones—the grasslands, the forests, the mountains—run north and south. What neither Mamie nor Ernest, nor 99 percent of the settlers heading into Palliser's Triangle understood, was that there are not one, but three distinctly different grasslands. The tallgrass prairie at the turn of the century took a bite out of southern Manitoba and stretched southward into parts of Nebraska, Kansas and Oklahoma (though the tallgrass prairie scarcely exists today).

A second grassland consisting of rough fescue (shortgrass) swings in a half moon from below the southern Alberta border upward, east into Saskatchewan, arcing protectively over part of the third grassland—the huge, diverse triangle of mixed-grass prairie that stretches from a point some 220 miles north of the Canadian border, growing spasmodically southward as far as Texas and covering the lion's share of the Great Central Plains.

The soil types within the mixed-grass prairie are mostly brown chernozemic—a rich, dark brown at the surface, but growing rapidly lighter as you go down, with a layer of lime carbonate not far below. The darker the soil, the richer it is, especially in the bottoms, where creeks flowed through coulees.

Wood Mountain, summer 1996. A young farmer, Rory Thomson, explains: "There's some of the best land anywhere down in these coulees. Three feet of topsoil. But on the hills in this unglaciated area, say from Willow Bunch to Horse Creek, the topsoil gets real thin."

Mamie was heading for the heart of Palliser's Triangle, a dryland region of predominantly light brown topsoil, well suited to grass and good for pastureland, so long as nobody messed with the structure of the sod, but a bad bet for monoculture cereal crops like the wheat they were planning to grow. The wild card in this triangle within the mixed-grass prairie was and still is the climate, for here is a region that routinely experiences searing heat and drought in the summer, extreme cold in the winter and almost continual wind. During July, temperatures above 100°F have been recorded here, and in

January, the coldest month, a reading of −45°F or −60° with wind-chill factored in.

The subtext to extreme climate is poor water supply. Rory Thomson's mom, Betty Thomson, remembers the stories of long droughts when livestock died of thirst: "The only redeeming factor here was the springs. The sloughs and creeks just dried up; so did a lot of wells."

Old Wives Lake, which Mamie would pass on her journey to the homestead, was a big body of water, but shallow and salty. It dried up twice, and although it still appears on most provincial maps as a good-sized lake, it has become a salty mudhole with a fitful water level. There are no major rivers flowing through the area. In wet years dozens of streams feed small lakes and sloughs, and where there are springs they're generally good ones, but in a dry year the evaporation rate increases, water levels drop quickly, and traditional sources— creeks, sloughs and wells—dry up completely.

A wheat crop is a fragile thing, relying on early moisture to germinate and continued moisture during the growing period—two conditions that often fail to coincide in the Wood Mountain region.

Mamie knew none of this, and there wasn't a lot she could have done about it anyway because her immediate future had already been decided and her duty was clear. She would follow Ernest. Like some latter-day Ruth, she believed the scriptures had clearly marked the path for women like her: "Whither thou goest I shall go, whither thou lodgest I shall lodge, thy people shall be my people forever. . . ." (It was one of her favorite passages from the Bible, and many years later, after my own father had announced that we were moving yet again, I heard her repeat it to my exasperated mother, who was near tears at the very idea of another move. When I married, the Song of Ruth was part of the ceremony at Pearl's suggestion. Though she didn't say so, I knew it was for Mamie.)

Given the rhetoric from the boosters, the Canadian government pamphlets and the Canada-or-bust euphoria that had seized her husband and his friends, what could Mamie say? She did as she was told and started packing.

This much Mamie knew: Her destination was somewhere on Section 34, Township 3, Range 3, west of the 3rd Meridian, in a country she'd never been to, in a province she couldn't pronounce. In *Cummin's Rural Directory* of 1922, I see the quarter sections marked with the family name, Harris, neatly handwritten by some long-gone civil servant.

Saskatchewan. I can hear her saying it over and over again, and no doubt she found it strangely musical, for even in her old age she would say it slowly, curling her tongue around the word, drawing the *a*'s out and treating them to her soft midwestern accent that would become so familiar to me.

The train goes to Moose Jaw, Ernest told her. *It's about eight hundred miles. Wood Mountain is somewhere south of that.* . . .

I've always imagined the two of them together in the kitchen, with a coal-oil lamp burning and a map of Canada spread on the table between them. My grandfather would be stabbing Moose Jaw with a forefinger, laughing at the name: *Moose Jaw! Whaddaya think of that for a name, Mamie?* And then running his thumb in a straight-as-the-crow-flies line southward, back toward the American border. *Wood Mountain Post is here someplace, just across the line, and we're south a few miles more, something between six and thirteen. You'll find it.*

In 1910 the map of Canada in their old American atlas ran out at Moose Jaw, the cartographer never having heard of place called Wood Mountain Post. (Wood Mountain Post had already made it onto the North-West Mounted Police map, where it sat near the end of a trail called the Old Pole Road.)

And the rain will follow the plow, Ernest told Mamie, quoting the words of the agrologist Cyrus Thomas. Surely this was one of the cruelest lies ever told to a dryland farmer. But then Ernest added his own mantra: *The wheat will grow like a weed.*

He said these things because he was a trusting optimist who genuinely believed the dryland prairie could be successfully farmed and because, like those other dream chasers who tried to turn Palliser's Triangle into wheat country, he didn't know any better.

ALTHOUGH SHE DIDN'T WRITE A FORMAL DIARY, Mamie kept her own kind of record in a green clothbound notebook with the words *Cash Book* printed rather grandly across the cover. There was a rich irony to that title, as she had so little cash to worry about, let alone to record. Her transactions were more tangible, and her Cash Book was full of recipes for making cakes, cheese, soap, and necessities— cough remedies, mustard plasters, whitewash—for it was around such homely and simple things that a country woman's daily routine was built. In her cash book she stored clippings, pressed flowers, jotted important notes and kept her endless lists, because she was an organized woman, serious about the business of homemaking, carefully noting the minutia of her domestic life. No jar of canned meat, no pickled beet or stewed plum went unrecorded in its season.

Livestock to be replaced was duly noted, as were the seeds planted each year, as were the birds added to her flocks of chickens and geese. She nursed a quiet passion for exotic poultry, and although she could never have afforded such a wildly extravagant purchase as a Bantam rooster just for the fun of owning one, she did keep a few Peking ducks as much for pleasure as for profit and once had an Iricana hen that laid green eggs and a Muscovy duck that had blue eyes and could flutter into low tree branches. (Long, long before my time, the blue-eyed duck and the hen that laid green eggs had disappeared into history, but Mamie brought them to life over and over again, until I could call them up simply by shutting my eyes.)

And so in this simple way, without ever calling it a diary, Mamie recorded her own history and that of her prairie homestead. Later, as she grew old, she and I were to become voracious column clippers, snipping items out of the *Family Herald* and the *Free Press Prairie Farmer.* Chickens and pigs in the *Herald's* full-color series on registered breeds were my favorites, while she favored pickle recipes or offers for a bigger, better tomato plant. Sadly, by that time her Cash Book, with all its ancient wisdom, had been retired to a bottom drawer.

Mamie's journey to Canada included one more essential: her round straw sewing basket. Her needles and thread, her small scissors and silver thimble, were in their way as important a piece of equipment as the Cash Book. Long before she could afford a sewing machine, every stitch of clothing her children wore and much of what she wore herself was patiently hand sewn. A farm woman sewed, mended and sewed again, and Mamie's sewing basket was almost as personal as her Cash Book.

The lid was oddly ornamented with a bunch of glass beads and a single brass Chinese coin with a squared-off hole in the middle, traditionally carried around on strings by merchants in old China. How she came by it I've no idea, but as a child I coveted that basket because of the beads—pink, blue and yellow—like a cluster of berries that had ripened unevenly. Their milky translucence turned them into sun catchers, and I remember wearing the lid as a hat with my most splendid dress-up garbs whenever she would let me. Today, the basket sits on my desk, near the Cash Book, its four remaining glass beads still attached by a faded red string to the old Chinese coin.

CHAPTER 4

A Place off the Map: 1911

*E*RNEST HAD PROMISED HER IT WASN'T
much of a trip, really—just eight hundred miles by train and then
double back by wagon to Wood Mountain. Mamie packed up her
household effects, such as they were, in two portions: one to take
along and one to send with Ernest. Among the take-alongs were two
books essential to Mamie's existence then and for as long as I knew
her: her Bible, and her Cash Book.

The day Mamie boarded the Soo Line coach, heading for the
unlikely sounding destination of Moose Jaw, she wasn't feeling well
and thought she might be getting the flu. But with three small children in tow—a six-year-old, a three-year-old and a nine-month-
old—she had little time to consider her own aches and pains.
Besides, she was pregnant again, so it was normal to feel a bit queasy.

She said good-bye to Ernest and her two older sons, and left
behind the friends and the few comforts she'd known in her first real
home, but if she had misgivings, she kept them to herself.

Along with her Bible, Cash Book and sewing box, she would

have packed a lunch for the overnight journey, but she'd also have needed diapers, baby blankets, bottles, all the bulky paraphernalia that young mothers are forced to drag around with them. She would have changed trains twice, once to the Northern Pacific and once again to the CPR. I wonder how she managed, this young woman with her children, and what her thoughts were as she watched the frontier unfold outside her window. I wonder too why she never told us about that trip and why I never asked. We became a train-traveling family thanks to my dad's railway pass, yet on those numerous occasions when my mother and Mamie packed a shoe box with our standard train lunch of egg salad sandwiches and boiled raisin cookies, I never heard a single word about what must have been her unforgettable journey to Canada.

Why didn't I ask?

This, at least, was reassuring: Ernest's friend Gurley Oakes would meet them in Moose Jaw and take them out to the homestead. Being met by a friend was of greater importance than even she realized because the frontier city with the funny name could be a wild and woolly place.

Moose Jaw has long since been tamed. Today, it's an attractive prairie city of treelined streets with its own mineral spa, an annual air show and a festival of marching bands that attracts thousands of visitors. But in the spring of 1911, it had attracted shady characters and high rollers, and if half of Moose Jaw put on airs and graces in their fancy brick houses, there was another part that made up for that by being poor, disreputable and faintly dangerous.

For a woman as sheltered as Mamie, one night among the bright lights of Moose Jaw would have been a rude awakening. Without a place to stay, with almost no money in her purse and with a reluctance to spend the little cash she had under any circumstances, the only thing within her means would have been a bed in one of the cheap hotels along River Street. There she'd have found herself and her children in the company of Moose Jaw's burgeoning population of prostitutes, country girls who had come into the big city to make their fortunes and ended up working the strip of seedy hotels—the Brunswick, the Empress, the American or the Alexandra. The hotels and a phalanx of poolrooms and billiard parlors—the Cecil, the Queen City, the Russell Pool Room, Riley's, the Colonial—were all within a few short blocks, all catering to young farmers who had a few bucks to spend whooping it up during their infrequent trips to town. She might have wandered into a grocery store called Yip Foo's with a poker game running in the basement and a few hookers operating from the rooms upstairs. Or possibly she'd have looked for a cheap meal in the Paris Cafe, where an opium den did a brisk business in a room behind the kitchen.

But none of that was necessary, and what might have been an adventure was averted because when the train pulled into Moose Jaw, Gurley Oakes was waiting for her. Tired, travel-worn, grubby and by now feeling like she had the flu, Mamie hustled her children onto Gurley's wagon box, even though it was already overloaded with lumber. It must have been an uncomfortable trip for the young woman with a baby on her knee and two other children that had to be tucked in somewhere among her bits of luggage.

From Moose Jaw it was a three-day journey over the Old Pole Road, which grew progressively rougher and narrower, becoming a sort of double-track goat trail as they traveled the 110 miles south from Moose Jaw to the Oakes homestead, near the place called Wood Mountain Post. It was unseasonably hot, and as the journey dragged into its second day Mamie felt progressively worse. They reached the Oakes homestead late on the third day, and after collapsing gratefully into the welcoming arms of the Oakes women, she miscarried. It would have been her seventh birth, and she was left weak, fragile and no doubt terrified at the very real possibility of dying and leaving her children motherless.

Mamie was spared the fate of many women who died in childbirth during the early years of settlement. No record of maternal deaths in Saskatchewan was kept prior to 1921, but in that year, a total of 128 maternal deaths were recorded, without regard to age or cause of death. In 1928, a year in which 123 women died in childbirth, 22 of them hemorrhaged to death, 53 died of miscellaneous infections, 11 died of "accidents during childbirth," two died of self-induced abortion and 20 died of kidney failure and convulsions.

As though her miscarriage wasn't trouble enough, there was Ernest and the older boys to worry about. She knew only that they expected to head north in their improvised wagon train on May 29, the day after she left. June days dragged into weeks, and there was no word. Then it was July 1, Canada's birthday, and still nothing. The other women tried to cheer her up, and while she helped with the housework they kept chirping away about the new homestead waiting for her. But Mamie had been too sick to go looking for it, and there was nothing there in any case, nor would there be unless her husband arrived soon. She was sure of only one thing: Until Ernest and her older sons appeared, she wouldn't have an easy hour or a decent night's sleep.

CHAPTER 5

The Dream Chasers

*Until all the desirable lands on the prairies
were fenced and claimed, the early settler's
philosophy, and reaction to loss of natural
resources was to use it up and move on.*
DONALD CHRISTISEN, *A Vignette of Native Prairie*

*M*EN LIKE ERNEST HARRIS, WHO
followed their dreams to the last best-west of Canada's interior dryland, the place we've learned to call Palliser's Triangle, saw before
them a new frontier. Yet it was anything but new. It had been inhab-
ited for millennia. The aboriginals who lived on the prairie grasslands, along with millions of buffalo (some sources have suggested
an original number as high as fifty million) lived in a place where, as
the centuries rolled along, time was marked only by the changing of
the seasons.

In the seventeenth century came the Europeans, the original
adventure tourists. The handful of fur traders and explorers who
made it as far as the prairies were a brave lot, but they never had any
intention of sticking around to put down roots and build communities. They had one goal and it was short term. I've always imagined
them writing postcards: *Dear Folks, This is a wild and desolate place. With
luck, we'll be home and dry before next Christmas.*

Eventually, two big trading companies hung out their shingles on the prairies, but although the North West Company and the Hudson's Bay Company were bitter rivals for the furs that kept them in business, they shared a profound disinterest in being stewards of the land and its resources. They were just passing through, and conservation was never an issue.

Between 1857 and 1860, John Palliser led a scientific expedition into the western interior for the Royal Geographical Society. He produced a voluminous report that divided the west into two great chunks: one fertile belt, which was roughly bounded by the North Saskatchewan River, and a smaller, triangular part to the south, which he described as arid plains. An even smaller portion within the triangle took up most of what is today the Wood Mountain region, extending all the way to the Cypress Hills. Palliser considered it a desert and probably a waste of time, so without bothering to explore it, he wrote it off as unfit for human habitation.

Meanwhile, between 1859 and roughly 1884, the Hudson's Bay Company posts at Fort Garry, Fort Qu'Appelle and the smaller posts at Wood Mountain and Cypress Hills were buying around ten thousand buffalo robes a year, adding up to some half million hides during that period. A business known simply as the American Fur Company consistently harvested even greater numbers south of the border, and some historians put the Hudson's Bay Company numbers much higher as well. Inevitably, this wholesale slaughter soon began to deplete the herds. In such a fragile, interdependent environment, a kind of domino effect is easily set off, and as Europeans began to affect buffalo habitats, species such as the plains grizzly and the swift fox began to disappear.

Large wolf packs that had followed the migrating buffalo met the same fate, and many thousands of wolves were poisoned by itinerant hunters known as wolfers, so named because it was their practice to lace a dead animal (frequently a buffalo carcass) with strychnine and swing back later to skin out the poisoned wolves and collect the hides. Wolfing was easy enough work, the profits were substantial, and by 1880 hunters had killed so many that the wolf had all but disappeared from its prairie habitat.

Within a remarkably short time, the ancient, peaceful prairies would be the silent witness to the near-extermination of several species, most notably the bison, who were scarce by 1878 and effectively wiped out by 1885, slaughtered in their millions. The ecosystem of the prairie was being rapidly and radically altered, and would never be the same again.

The encroaching Europeans wanted the hides or the thrill of the kill, and in some cases they wanted the land traditionally occupied by nomadic aboriginals, for which they were quite prepared to starve them out. There is no clear agreement among historians over which of these reasons bore the greatest weight in what was, in the end, an ecological disaster and what became for the aboriginals who had relied on the hunt a social chaos from which they would never recover.

The traders had not come west empty-handed. As guns and cheaply concocted alcohol, known colloquially as fire-water, was distributed to aboriginals, all hell broke loose on the grasslands. The effects of alcohol on the Indians were disastrous, a fact well known by the white men who brewed it for them. The following recipe, handwritten, was found in the records of a druggist, John D. Higinbotham of Lethbridge, Alberta, and was evidently the one used by whiskey traders from Fort Benton, Montana. The original document, scrawled on the bottom of a handwritten note in 1899, now resides in the Glenbow Institute, in Calgary.

Fort Whoop-Up Recipe for the liquor traded to Indians:
Rx alcohol (S.P.R) 1 *qt.*
black strap chewing tobacco—1 lb.

Jamaica ginger—1 bottle
Black molasses—1 quart
water—q.s.
The whole boiled until "ripe"
A cup of the above for one buffalo hide.

The dream chasers who burst so eagerly upon the prairies at the turn of the century were at the dawn of an era, but for the original inhabitants of the plains, a hunting and gathering society that had relied on the bison since their first hunters appeared on this land, a long, dark night was falling. They were no longer a proud and independent people, and all that remained for them was subjugation and humiliation. In years to come, a few of these people would become well known to Mamie.

During her brief stop in Moose Jaw, she naturally had no time for sightseeing. If she had, she might have noticed the scattering of tents down by the creek. They were families of Hunkpapa Sioux, the last remnants of the larger tribe of Teton Sioux, followers of Chief Sitting Bull. One of the men was called Big Joe, and his path would cross Mamie's many times. Although she'd grown up in mortal fear of Indians during her childhood on the Great Plains, she would come to like and respect Big Joe and his family, and consider them friends.

Big Joe would have been a little boy when the Battle of the Little Big Horn was fought, but his father was a warrior, and during the sound and fury of General Custer's much-ballyhooed last stand, little Joe was probably hiding somewhere nearby, scared half to death.

In 1877, the year Mamie was born, Sitting Bull had managed to lead several thousand of his bedraggled people, including that little boy, across the border into the sanctuary of the Wood Mountain. Although the Hunkpapa were a nomadic subtribe who had originally made their living as buffalo hunters, by the time Mamie arrived they'd been reduced to a small band under Black Bull, spending most of their year encamped along the river in Moose Jaw. It was said that Big Joe had fought in the Riel Rebellion and had returned to Moose Jaw after the humiliating defeat of the Métis and the execution of the man who had become a kind of surrogate chief. Eventually, Joe would wander back to Wood Mountain and make a living traveling the district as an itinerant butcher, which took him occasionally to Ernest's farm and into Mamie's kitchen.

"Big Joe would be at the farm to see Ernest about one thing or another," Mamie recalled, "and sometimes he'd stay for a meal. We was always happy to see him. I never had a finer gentleman set up to my table."

THE DAY AFTER MAMIE SET OUT for Wood Mountain, her husband and two older sons had turned their backs on the Nebraska farmstead and headed north. They packed a covered wagon with a few of her dishes, her stew pot, cast-iron frying pan, copper wash boiler and a washboard. A two-seat, heavy-wheeled buggy, known as a democrat, was tagged on behind. The democrat was loaded with the rest of Mamie's earthly goods and her collection of cackling poultry: two dozen laying hens, a cantankerous old rooster, three turkeys and three geese.

The geese were her special project. She had managed to hatch them in a nest of flannel tucked behind the kitchen stove and had nursed and petted them along until they grew strong and sassy. Now she had two white females and a handsome gray gander that would get her flock started once they got to Wood Mountain. Along with her carefully hoarded garden seeds (their varieties meticulously noted in the Cash Book) these birds were Mamie's stake in her Canadian future.

Ernest's four horses were hitched to the covered wagon, which he drove. Roy, who was ten, rode in the wagon, and Roly, nearly fourteen, followed on his pony, leading their biggest investment, a big, black Percheron stallion for which Ernest had swapped most of his one section of Nebraska land. The Percheron, a heavy draft horse that could pull a plow, would be invaluable once they started breaking land on the virgin prairies of Saskatchewan. The thick grass everybody called prairie wool would require a deep furrow, and that big horse was their stake in the future.

The contemporary map of the American Midwest with its long, gray lines of high-speed interstates leads the traveler smoothly north, past the Days Inns, Howard Johnsons, Denny's and Chickin' Lickin's, past the drive-through restaurants, lube and gas shops, car washes and banks, and all the myriad comforts for people on four wheels. Ernest's route was a little more challenging. In tracing that journey on the map in my head, I see them traveling by one recommended trail or another into South Dakota, through Wounded Knee and along the Cheyenne River, skirting the Black Hills where they'd have run into spring storms, guiding horses and wagons across a dozen nameless streams and at least one broad river. Somewhere along the Cheyenne they'd have turned northwest, crossed the Little Missouri, and in a few days of fine weather chewed off the bottom corner of North Dakota and again swung hard west into Montana, crossing the Powder River and reaching for the Yellowstone River at Miles City.

Roly, riding his pony, was supposed to lead the prized Percheron stallion all the way across the line into Canada, but a day or so before Miles City the big horse slowed noticeably and was off his feed. My grandfather didn't just trade horses, he loved them in an unsentimental way, reveling in their strength, respecting them as co-workers on his land. Unlike so many western men who lived by the blood and sweat of their animals, he never mistreated any horse he owned, and when he saw that the big Percheron was in a bad way, he decided they should spend a night in a livery stable to let the animal rest up.

That's where they met John Ashbaugh, a stranger who seemed to be in a tearing hurry to get into Canada and wanted traveling companions. There was something about Ashbaugh that Ernest liked, and his gut feeling was to trust the stranger, although he must have suspected the reason for a lone traveler to be in such a rush to cross the Canadian border.

The next day the two men and the boys headed out from Miles City, making camp a couple of nights later at Cat Creek, but it had become painfully clear that the big black horse was too weak to go on. Roly was left behind with a sick horse and a stranger with a price on his head while Ernest and his younger son traveled on without them.

Cat Creek must have been a placid little stream on a good day, for it was too small to make it onto any of the major maps. I see it bending and twisting through a coulee in a leisurely way, winking in the sunlight, rippling over smooth brown stones in the shallows and shaded by overhanging willows where it ran deeper. It would have offered refuge to speckled trout and the odd passerby who might water his horse and even bathe, if he had time to pause. Like many streams, this one had another side to its nature, and a sudden cloudburst breaking over Cat Creek could turn it mean and ugly.

A few years before my Uncle Roly died, he read from a memoir he'd written for inclusion in a Wood Mountain history book while I listened to the unfolding memory of an old man reaching backward, struggling to touch those places and events he'd almost forgotten.

"It rained that night and all the next day. My, didn't it rain! It just poured down, like Noah's flood. Cat Creek turned itself into a river and rose so high and so fast we couldn't cross it anywhere. If we tried, I'd lose the stallion, and maybe my pony. . . . We were just stuck.

"The next day I think it was, the stallion up and died. I knew it would break Pop's heart to lose that horse, and I felt so bad I like as near cried."

The bottomlands along a creek bed are often black and rich, and settlers who knew what they were doing built as near the creek as they safely could. A rancher on Cat Creek befriended the kid with the sick horse, and after the water went down he helped Roly make a pack for his pony, gave him a slab of bacon, some canned beans and bread, and once again Mamie's eldest son and his companion, the mysterious John Ashbaugh, headed for the border. With the rain behind them it wasn't long before they got a taste of what the high, hot sun of late June can do to the prairie.

"You could have fried eggs on a rock," Uncle Roly said. "John's feet got sore. His socks wore out. His feet blistered something terrible. His boots hurt him awful. I never saw worse blistered feet. Then we run out of water. An Indian boy come along the trail, and we asked how far it was to water, so he pointed the way, and we walked on."

In the relentless heat, there was considerable danger of a prairie fire. Anything could start it: lightning, a careless smoker, even a spark from a horse's shoe striking a stone. Or the Indians might be starting their annual burns. The plains had become a place of dwindling resources for those who had by long tradition made their living off the land, and now the Métis and what remained of the Cree and Blackfoot routinely set small fires so buffalo bones, a valuable commodity, could more easily be seen.

William Least Heat-Moon, writing about the Kansas grasslands in *PrairyErth*, called that well-known prairie quartet of tornado, grasshopper, drought and fire the four horsemen of the prairie, but of all four, said Moon, the greatest of these is fire: "a rider with two faces because for everything taken it makes a return in equal measure."

That may be true, except that it's not the two-faced rider, but the structure of the grass itself that makes the return possible. Grass is the most abundant plant on the face of the earth. Over one hundred varieties thrive in the shortgrass and mixed-grass prairie, adapting amiably to extremes of climate, terrain and soil type, and relying on its vast root system to get maximum use from every drop of water that comes its way. Its thick, ridged leaves resist evaporation, and its hollow stem and thick joints will bend in the wind without breaking. But here is the miraculous part, the special characteristic that allows it to survive: Because it grows from its base slightly below ground, rather than from its tip, grass withstands almost any trauma, including fire, close cropping by hungry animals, even the repeated beating of hooves. And it seems to come back with renewed vigor.

All that said, a grass fire travels like the wind and destroys everything in its path. Under no circumstances could Roly and his companion risk even the smallest cooking fire, so for the next two days they ate their food cold. Then they ran out of everything except the bacon, and at the hungry end of yet another sweltering day, Roly opened the sack and made a discovery.

"The bacon was real wet. When I put my hand in the sack, it felt kind of slimy, and when I pulled out the slab, well . . . maggots. The bacon was squirming with maggots. It made me sick. Still does, just thinking about it."

But man and boy had to eat, and there was nothing else. Magdalena would have understood: On her journey, she'd likely choked down her share of maggoty bacon.

During the interview, Uncle Roly, who is eighty-something as we speak, shakes his head, closes his eyes. I'm taping his story, and he asks me to turn off the tape recorder. It's as though having eaten the infested meat, he'd done something shameful, or maybe sinful (he'd been a born-again Christian since his early twenties, and even an imagined sin weighed heavily on his shoulders). I remind him that what I'm writing isn't fiction, but hopefully a true account of several journeys, including his own, and this is part of his truth. He agrees then, but asks me not to dwell on it.

"When we crossed West Poplar Creek, the road divided, so we took the most used branch. Of course it was the wrong one. It led to Willow Bunch. Eventually, we come out on the Willowvale Flat. . . . There was a few little shacks, but nobody around. Finally, we come to where a man was at home. He set us straight. Wood Mountain was twenty miles straight across, going northwest."

By the time Roly led his loaded pony and his sore-footed friend onto the Harris homestead, the fourteen-year-old boy had walked 140 miles. Ernest and Roy had arrived just two days before. It was July 6, 1911, and Mamie had her family together again.

Unknown to Ernest, there was a warrant out for gentle John Ashbaugh in several states and a dead-or-alive reward in at least one, or so he'd told his fourteen-year-old companion during the journey. That may be why he faded from family and local history as soon as he reached Canada. Uncle Roly told me about the warrant, although, believing that a man is innocent until proven guilty, he refused to say what crimes Ashbaugh was supposed to have committed. Whatever yarns were told around the campfire, my uncle kept them to himself.

"John Ashbaugh was a good man," he told me. And added in a low and thoughtful voice attached to some memory I'd have given a lot to tap, "Yessir, turned out real good in the end."

CHAPTER 6

An Ordinary Woman

$\mathcal{T}$HE MEN WHO SETTLED THE WEST have always enjoyed considerable attention from the literary world and the press, who saw them as romantic swashbucklers, courageously building a future on a wild frontier. Much less has been said about the women who followed them and who, in some cases such as in Mamie's, actually arrived ahead of them.

Local history books noted the presence of wives and daughters in specific families, and devoted an occasional paragraph or two of tribute to the kindness, forbearance and culinary skills of these women. But even when it was the women who were doing the writing, or maybe because of it, recorded history has focused predominantly on the men. With few notable exceptions, traditional western fiction writers have also chosen to ignore ordinary women. It's true that popular American mythology paid tribute to the Annie Oakleys and Calamity Janes, but their fame was based on their ability to compete with men in ridin', ropin' and shootin', all the while retaining their girlish figures and never surrendering their virginity.

Mamie Elizabeth Harris, although a competent horsewoman, was no Annie Oakley, nor did she have the advantage of a well-off family or a good education. She was by any standards an ordinary woman. She never finished school, and although she was an avid reader while her eyesight lasted, and was able to do simple arithmetic, she was never taught the concept of numerical progression. The pages in her handwritten Cash Book are numbered, but page 101 is written 1001, 126 is 10026 and so on. She never worked for wages or had a penny of her own that hadn't first passed through the hands of her father, her husband or, later, her male children. Even her old age pension cheque came at the behest of a man. It was 1916 before she was allowed to vote in a provincial election and 1918 before she voted federally.

Historians are fond of suggesting that the western suffrage movement thrived because of a supportive and politically progressive rural male populace who saw their wives as equal partners. Farm organizations such as the Saskatchewan Grain Growers Association did support the suffragettes, but why would they not? The women's vote considerably beefed up the total rural vote and gave the sparsely populated West the additional political clout it needed. For farmers, female suffrage made good business sense.

Until 1929 Mamie was not even considered a person under Canadian law. She was a chattel. When I was in high school, I looked that word up in my dictionary and discovered that it meant "a possession that could be moved." Even if she'd wanted to, she was legally forbidden to enter a beer parlor, a circumstance that remained until the late fifties, when the law changed to allow for "ladies and escorts."

Mamie was never politically active, and although she worked hard for her church and community, she was not known and is not remembered as a leader. She had little leisure time, so the things she coveted were not for herself, but for her children—mostly, she wanted a better education for them, especially for her daughters.

For every Nellie McClung or Hilda Neatby who appeared on the western scene with intellectual guns blazing, there were thousands of Mamies. It seems to me that most of what has been written about these ordinary women leans toward two extremes. One is the standard good-old-days account jotted into community cookbooks and local histories— rose-tinted memories of feathery biscuits, happy quilting bees and Sunday school picnics, when everybody was a good neighbor and even the meanest drunk in the territory was really just a rough diamond. The other extreme is the grim, sad memoir of wasted lives and too-early deaths.

Probably the truth about the lives of most rural women who came to the prairies as pioneers is neither as innocently merry nor as depressingly dreadful as these accounts suggest. Judging by Mamie's own life and the way it unfolded, I believe the truth rests somewhere in the middle. Solitary and exhausting though their lives may have been, the women who stuck it out on the frontier formed a bond with the western prairies that would last a lifetime and be passed down the generations, from mother to daughter to granddaughter.

Why hasn't more been written about the role of the ordinary rural woman in the West? Maybe because her frontier-bred, grin-and-bear-it tradition didn't allow for public soul-bearing. To complain about anything more personal than the weather would have been an admission of weakness or defeat, and it wasn't done. On the other hand, a woman had to be cautiously circumspect about even her smallest personal victories because to talk about them might be construed as tooting her own horn, and that wasn't done either. Modesty, like frugality and the work ethic, was an essential virtue in a good farm woman. There was a certain discretion in women's interpersonal relationships, and among Mamie's peers, the details that would today be considered mere juicy tidbits were not routinely trotted out for group discussion over the teacups, not even among sisters or between mothers and daughters. It's probably true that such discretion was part innocence, part ignorance because their vocabulary didn't cover even basic human anatomy, let alone human sexuality.

The bizarre or painful aberrations that now and then turned into nasty family secrets—brutality, drunkenness, infidelity, incest, unwanted pregnancies, botched abortions, the whole litany of essentially female woes that keeps the contemporary analyst's phone ringing—remained a secret, except under the most extreme circumstances.

I remember the chilly reception I got from my mother when I published what I thought was an honestly reflective and affectionate essay about her sister Nell, my twice-divorced, thrice-married California aunt, some twenty years after her death. It is probably what stops me now from relating the circumstances surrounding at least one of those divorces, the fascinating details of which were kept secret until after the aunt's death, in the permissive sixties. Although American divorce law was more enlightened, a Canadian woman trying to get out of a bad marriage faced so many legal, religious and social barriers that it was seldom worth the effort. Adultery, whether real or staged, had to be cited, and divorce was an automatic scandal.

Had Mamie not married, her life would have been considered incomplete, at least by others if not by herself. The dreaded specter of the pathetic old maid haunted all but the most independent women and was responsible for some desperately bad matches that might have been laughable had they not been so tragic. To be a single woman after thirty was to be not quite good enough, to be left on the shelf, the butt of bad jokes, always aware that somewhere down the road waited the ultimate indignity of a dependent old age. The unmarried woman would become a burden to a married sister or niece, shuttled from family to family, living as a permanent intruder, the rather tiresome and not-quite-welcome guest in someone else's home.

Although urban matrons seem to have had a few more luxuries, more leisure and a certain amount of social status in communities where they could bask in the reflected glory of successful husbands, the rural woman had a different agenda. Her marriage wasn't about status, happiness or self-fulfillment. Quite simply, it was about survival.

Mamie was a survivor, and I wonder now if those skills of somehow keeping your head above water even if you aren't much of a swimmer can, through some obscure process of genetic imprinting, be inherited or if they must be learned.

IN MARRYING A FARMER, Mamie declared herself to have a strong work ethic and unquenchable optimism. Like thousands of ordinary farm women, she bought into a package deal that would include mothering, cooking, sewing, gardening, milking cows, feeding pigs and managing a flock of laying hens. Had she been a city girl, Mamie might have envisioned such a job description along with a pastoral existence in a ruffled apron and a sunbonnet, with strawberry socials in July and a bountiful, dashing-through-the-snow Christmas to brighten the long winter.

But Mamie was one hundred percent country, and she could read the fine print. For a farm woman, marriage was domestic service, pure and simple; home nursing too, and pinch-hitting for the hired man her husband needed but couldn't afford. Sometimes it meant fighting prairie fires with a wet pillowcase or watching her garden freeze black the second week of August or pulling a calf in the middle of the night to help a cow through a hard labor and then maybe losing the calf. Or having her teeth ache and rot off because there was no dentist within seventy miles and no money even if he'd been just a quick hop down the trail. It meant giving birth too often and watching children do without shoes, education or medical care. Sometimes, with the children, it meant watching them die. The rural woman's personal creed of making do and getting by or, in its less genteel form, putting up and shutting up, was to endure for the first half of the twentieth century.

More fine print: along with the relentless physical labor went the loneliness and isolation, the harsh climate, the ever-present keening of the wind. Cabin fever was not invented in modern suburbia—it was a prairie ailment long before it had a name, and the dreadful sameness of her daily life could break a woman's spirit. The few without the mental or emotional strength to cope with it simply gave up.

In the summer of 1996, in the kitchen of a Saskatchewan ranch tucked so far back in the hills that even today people scarcely know it's there, I watch a woman named Rachel pour strong tea into a mug with a half-inch of canned milk in the bottom and stir in a generous spoonful of sugar. Her walnut-colored hand shoves a plate of warm cookies across the table and she says, "Take two—they're small." I know these cookies. They're called hermits, and when I bite into one the flavors of nutmeg, currants and walnuts come together in a familiar way, evoking another kitchen, when I was a kid. Mamie made hermits, and so did my mother, and I ate them by the fistful after school and on Saturdays, when I came home freshly humiliated from my weekly piano lesson. Hermits are prairie food, embellished with the dried fruit and nuts that were available in all seasons to people who lived in isolated places.

Rachel, who will be ninety on her next birthday or maybe ninety-one (there seems to be some question about this) has lived her entire life in these hills, including the dust-bowl days of the thirties that nearly finished off her family's fledgling ranch. She figures she knows what lonesome looks like. Always has.

"Weeks on end, you'd never see another woman. Nobody to talk to. Just that infernal wind blowin' the dust around. The wind could play tricks on your ears, especially at night, if you was alone. It could drive you batty."

She picks up the mug in both hands, and I can't help noticing the arthritic knuckles.

"I remember once—I was ten or eleven I guess, pretty young anyway—a woman over by Assiniboia went batty. Hanged herself in the barn. Climbed into the loft, put a rope around her neck, tied it to the rafter and jumped. Husband come home a day or two later, found her hanging there. Three little kids hardly more than babies, all howling away, scared and hungry. Kids is smart, even little ones—they know when something's not right. Well, anyhow, he sent the kids back east. Couple of years later, he disappeared. Went across the line, folks said."

It would be the midfifties before one simple event—the introduction of electricity into rural Saskatchewan—would work a dramatic change in the lives of prairie farm women, reducing their isolation and cutting their manual labor almost in half. Electricity may have come late to this part of the world, but when it arrived it was a veritable grab bag of luxuries, of dripless refrigerators whirring contentedly, and freezers that finally halted the relentless canning. Washing machines—no more rubbing your knuckles raw on a washboard. Electric cream separators—no more cranking the handle. And such lights! Lights that came on with the flick of a switch, so no more oil lamps smoking up the house, no more chimneys to wash, wicks to trim, mantles to replace, no more lanterns getting tipped over in the barn. "And no more of them heavy old sad irons clunking around on their wooden handles, scorching your best blouse 'cause they was too danged hot." So said Rachel.

The ultimate luxury was an electric stove with burners and an oven that operated independently, oblivious to the whim of damp wood or smoking coal, and never an ash pan to empty. Still, Rachel has a small wood burning stove in her kitchen, which she uses for her weekly batch of bread, winter and summer.

"I figure the electric stove was good for everything but bread. With bread, you'd get loaves falling every danged time, and the crust tougher 'n boot leather."

Long before the electric miracle revolutionized the working lives of rural women, Mamie was stolidly, faithfully playing out the hand she'd been dealt. She had her own dreams and was, in her way, an independent woman. Twice she packed up her children and traveled, alone and far away, to arrive in a new place ahead of her husband. During her lifetime she lived under two flags, through five wars, in three American states and two Canadian provinces, and she gave birth to nine children.

In one way, Mamie was luckier than many women of her time and place because she married for love. By all accounts, it was a love that endured until her husband's death in 1947.

Doby House:
A Home of Her Own

They had found high grass. . . . There were good sized trees and shrubs or
small brush, also wild fruit, pin cherries, saskatoons and wild red raspberries,
also highbush cranberries. There were springs of wonderful water, and because
of the lush growth . . . the men felt sure good crops would grow here.
—MRS. GURLEY OAKES, They Came to Wood Mountain

"HERE," FOR MAMIE, WAS ON THE bank of a coulee somewhere south of Wood Mountain Post and only a few hundred yards from the ridge that marked the continental divide, so that all the water from Mamie's side of the ridge flowed south into the Missouri River while all the water on the other side went north toward Hudson Bay.

Mamie's first house, known among the family women as "the mud house" but described by the uncles in slightly grander terms as adobe, or simply "doby," was no palace by any standards. A single room, it measured 14x16' the first year, and although it would grow slightly larger with rooms added here and there over the next few years as the family grew, it was, according to Uncle Ken, never a comfortable or convenient house.

"They built on a coulee, which was at first a disadvantage. There were some winters with a lot of snow, and the northwest wind would blow in and drift right over the buildings, up ten or fifteen feet. . . . Other winters, we had hardly any snow at all."

The roof of the doby house was low and curved, rather than peaked and eaved, so the winds swooping low over the prairie would have less to grab. The framework was of diamond willow poles cut from the coulee, placed side by side and plastered with a wet mud made of a mixture of local clay and prairie wool.

My mother told me stories about the small, low-ceilinged rooms of the doby house she only half-remembered, but for Mamie the house was always real and important. It was her first home in Canada, built partly with her own two hands, and her nesting instinct took over. I could imagine her chirping away: *We need some beds, Ernest, and a table. . . . Those nail kegs will make good stools, when I cover them with cheese-cloth. . . .*

This wouldn't have been considered a large number of household effects, but with two adults, five children, a couple of dogs and the essential mouser-cat, she had a roomful.

It was too late to plant a crop that first year, so Ernest got a job hauling freight to Moose Jaw, a trip that took ten days in good summer weather, a lot longer in bad weather or snow. But it paid well, a dollar for a hundred pounds, and they couldn't afford to turn down money like that.

Left on her own again, Mamie surveyed her new kingdom and decided she needed a chicken house for her poultry, which had traveled remarkably well from Nebraska and were residing in temporary pens. The older boys were assigned the task of digging a hole in the side of the hill for her chickens and geese, and shoring it up so it would be snug and secure from chicken-stealing coyotes.

As soon as they'd finished, she put them to work digging a root cellar under the mud house (Mamie called it a *ruut* cellar) to keep butter and milk cool and store the potatoes she now needed to find to feed her family. Next year there would be vegetables to store, bushels and bushels of potatoes, carrots, turnips, just as soon as she could get her seeds planted, get a garden going. She could almost see her garden stretching out in the prairie sunshine, and by this time next year she'd be able to lay on a real feast for Ernest and the kids and whatever guests might come down the trail, but for now she had little time to dream.

The house had to be winterized, so she set the boys to building an outer wall with more diamond willow poles, insulating the wall space with prairie wool, filling in the chinks with cellar mud and plastering over that layer with more prairie adobe, which gave it a smooth and remarkably weatherproof finish. In Uncle Roly's notes I read: "That was a good house. Warm as could be. We all seven of us lived in it that winter. We had an old cast-iron stove Dad got in Moose Jaw for two dollars—it didn't look like much, but it kept us warm."

Whatever the deficiencies of the mud house, at least Mamie was spared a soddy, the sod shack used by so many settlers in the region. While sod was a good insulator against heat, cold and the ever-present wind, sod roofs leaked like sieves when it rained and continued to drip long after a storm had passed. The worst things about sod houses were the bugs, mice and snakes that lived in the earth, an accepted hazard of such living quarters. According to a woman whose mother lived in a one-room sod house for twelve years, the experience was distinctly thin on charm:

"Those women had such a terrible time. They were damp, dirty places. Bed bugs, head lice, rats, mice. Some say they were snug, but I don't know about that—some of the shacks were so cold that they used to take the bread dough to bed so it would be warm enough to rise."

Chapter 8

Waiting for Ernest

B Y THE FIRST WEEK OF AUGUST, with the help of some neighbors, Ernest and the older boys had built a barn, and they'd found good water on the first try at digging their well. But the summer was flying, and he and Mamie both knew that this winter, their first, would be a hard one, maybe the hardest they'd ever experienced. If what they'd heard of Saskatchewan winters proved even halfway true, they were heading into a long, lean, isolating season, and he had to make some money fast, before it hit.

He'd head north, taking with him eight recently traded horses. Heavy horses were in demand among the incoming settlers—they were essential for breaking the land, and if Ernest knew anything, he knew good horseflesh. His plan was to trade four horses and keep the best four as a team, hiring out as part of a mobile threshing crew. After that, he'd do some freighting, maybe some carpentry—he could turn his hand at almost anything. When they said good-bye, neither he nor Mamie had any real notion of when they would be together again or how she would manage the family and the homestead in his absence.

At home with the two older boys and three younger children, Mamie coped as best she could, and as they all grew accustomed to the prairie, the long, hot days of August ran together in a not unpleasant way. Mamie walked with the little ones through the meadow south of their house, where Ernest's wheat would grow next year, and they picked berries up and down the coulee. They picked flowers too, sweet rocket and purple asters, queen anne's lace and goldenrod, and took home bouquets for the kitchen table. The wildflowers brightened the place, and until she could have her own flower garden they'd do nicely.

One afternoon there was something different, something strange, and at first she couldn't decide what it was. The day was so hot, with a sharp, metallic quality in the air, and there was an odd stillness, as though the prairie was holding its breath. Then she saw it, the dirty yellow haze in the southwest, and before long she could smell the smoke, and the stillness of the day was gone as a high-pitched wind howled up from the west. She'd heard horror stories about prairie fires and had seen the results of them through the train windows as she traveled through the Dakotas. She knew that if the wind turned even slightly, this one would be on top of them within hours.

Ernest had cut all their tallgrass, the bluestem that made such good hay, but it was growing up again, and no fireguard had been plowed around their buildings. A neighbor rode by, but he could only stop long enough to warn her to fill every barrel, every pitcher and bowl with water, and take them to the edge of the tallgrass. He showed her how to light a backfire if she had to, and then he was gone. When darkness fell, she drew her children together and they watched in horrified fascination as the western sky turned red, reflecting the flames that were moving ever closer. Mamie was a religious woman, and I suppose she prayed harder that night than she ever had before, then wondered why she still felt helpless and downright scared.

Mamie didn't know it, but she was smack in the middle of an area known for its terrible grass fires. Only two years before, in 1909, the entire country between Wood Mountain and the Canadian Pacific main line had burned, killing two people and great numbers of cattle and horses. Had she been able to see into the future, she'd have known to expect devastating fires in their still sparsely plowed region in 1915 and the next two years.

In those years, in worse fires than this one, Mamie would drive a stoneboat along the fire lines with barrels of water, bumping over the stubble, ignoring the burning in her throat, choking on the smoke that filled her lungs and stung her eyes, and in all of this she would not flinch. Controlling her terrified horse with difficulty, she would drive up and down the line again and again while the men fighting the fire dipped their gunnysacks and went back to their futile gestures of beating at the flames. Later she would watch, helpless, as the fire leapt the fireguard and devoured their pastures with their high, sweet crops of winter hay. Later still it would come again, the prairie fire, and that time it would take their wheat.

But on this day the prairie wasn't yet ready to test her. By morning the fire had gone around, as though to give her fair warning that it would be back and the next time she wouldn't be so lucky or get off so easily.

Mid-September and still no sign of Ernest. At night, when the children were asleep and the walls of the little house seemed to close in on her, how small and helpless my grandmother must have felt, and how alone. Too exhausted to sleep, she would alternately count her blessings and worry, and fire off a short prayer whenever it seemed appropriate.

Blessings: healthy children, roof over their heads, Ernest. *Lord, bring him home soon.*

Worries: *Where was Ernest? What if something had happened to him? What if he doesn't come home at all?*

Mamie wasn't afraid of the dark, but she didn't like it either and told me that the worst thing about prairie winters wasn't the cold, but the long nights. As September became October and the days grew shorter and still Ernest hadn't appeared, her vague unease turned to fear.

Those long, wind-howling, owl-hooting, coyote-yelping prairie nights were enough to bring out the sissy in any greenhorn, let alone a young woman with five children to care for. Such nights pushed some women to the brink of madness, and Mamie was no eager heroine. She felt her own vulnerability, and she feared for her children. When darkness fell, her list of daytime worries was compounded. What was that scratching noise? Was the livestock all right, or had a fox gotten into the chicken pen? Listen! Were those hoofbeats she heard? Was that a light moving out there to the east? The border was so close. She'd heard stories about outlaws crossing the line, dangerous men on the run. No, don't be silly. There's nobody out there. It must be her imagination. Let it be her imagination. . . . Mamie would give herself a mental shake and force her tired head back onto the pillow, to listen to the rhythmic breathing of her children and wait for the gray fingers of dawn to peel back the night and come slipping through her window.

THE ABSENCE OF LIGHT can play tricks on the human mind. For centuries people's innate fear of the dark has been used successfully by captors to bring prisoners in solitary confinement to a state of incoherent raving.

I admit that I've always shared Mamie's fear of the dark. Once, staying alone in an old house in Italy, I spent a night scared stiff, my fear generated by the creaking and groaning of an ancient building protesting a recently installed heating system. I heard footsteps on the stairs, heard the door creak open, heard feet patter across the floor. But the worst thing was the thick, almost palpable darkness of the shuttered room. I felt disoriented, my pulse raced, my heart thumped, and mature adult that I was, I covered my head with the sheet and held my breath.

WHEN SUNRISE ARRIVED at the end of one of those long, lonely nights, Mamie realized that she had a bigger problem: She was rapidly running out of food. The hens had stopped laying. Without her usual mammoth garden, she had nothing to fall back on, and Ernest had left her so little money that even if she'd had access to a grocer, every cent would have been considered twice before she spent it.

A neighbor had earlier sold her twenty-five bushels of potatoes at one dollar per bushel, and she still had a sack of flour, so for a while she fed the children bread and potatoes. Potato bread, plain fried potatoes, boiled potatoes, hashbrown potatoes, potato cakes with leftover potatoes, potato pancakes with fresh potatoes, potato dumplings, spaetzle made with potatoes, and when every other culinary possibility available to a cook with an empty larder had been explored and exhausted, she made potato soup. Ken, her youngest son, remembers an all-purpose gravy made of browned flour and water to go with almost every dish.

(At infrequent gatherings of her daughters during Mamie's old age, one of my aunts used to enrage her by insisting that there were times in those early years and later, in the hard times, when she'd been "hungry enough to eat soap," and Mamie would get all huffy and fire back that her children may not have had many luxuries, but they always had enough to eat, *always,* and they were never hungry, *never.*)

And still Ernest stayed away.

When the flour ran out and there were only enough potatoes left for one more meal, Mamie said one more prayer and told Roly to get on his pony and ride to the North-West Mounted Police at Wood Mountain Post. The Mounted Police had been her ally ever since she crossed the border. Like Sitting Bull and his people before her, she trusted the redcoats, and in any case she was desperate enough to forget whatever pride might have kept her from asking for help. By suppertime, Roly was riding up to the house with one hundred pounds of flour across his saddle. A few days later a Mountie came by with chicken feed for her poultry.

That wasn't the last time the North-West Mounted Police helped her family with food. One officer or another stopped by frequently on routine patrols from Wood Mountain Post, checking to see that the family was indeed surviving, and they seemed to know when Mamie was running short. If they stayed for a meal, they paid for it, waving away her protests, assuring her that it was covered by expenses. Magically, an extra sack of flour would appear in one of the freight loads Ernest hauled for them, or a side of bacon, and it would be handed over with the face-saving assurance that some careless supply sergeant had sent too much of this or that, so if she could use it she'd be doing them a favor.

It may have been that first winter that gave Mamie her lifelong affection and respect for the decent, compassionate lawmen that she first knew at Wood Mountain Post and who were eventually to become the Royal Canadian Mounted Police. Throughout her life, if any slighting remark about the Mounties was made in her hearing, she took it personally. She'd have gone to the wall to defend them.

November, now. Still no word from Ernest. *Where was he?* On the morning when Mamie looked out the window and saw snow on the ground, her heart sank. *Wasn't it too early for snow?* Snow was another season. Snow was winter. Again the prairie began to tease her, blowing up freak storms at midday, just a few snowflakes at first, and then would come the graying of the light, the flakes falling faster, heavier. And so the prairie flexed its muscles with an early blizzard that left her isolated in the doby house, unable to see ten feet outside the window, afraid to let the boys go to the barn for chores in case they couldn't find their way back.

A winter on those southern prairies can be almost snow free. Oh, it'll still be cold enough to freeze the creeks, and the wind will still blow most of the time, and every morning there's a silvery sheen of frost on the brown hills, but as winters go, it's not bad. In a hard winter, one with early snow and a lot of it, the season acquires texture and dimension, measured in the height of drifts and the depth to which the temperatures fall.

During Mamie's first winter there was often ice fog in the mornings, and when the sun broke through she'd see the hoarfrost hanging thick on the scrawniest twig, and even a bunch of weeds poking through the snow would twinkle and wink in the sunshine like cut crystal. At that moment, winter was a work of art.

But later, when the wind took over and a blizzard blew in, there was trouble like she'd never known in any winter she could recall. It often seemed to start in the afternoon, when the light was about to fade anyway, and she'd see the snow blowing off an open field and then across the trail, so it looked like smoke rolling along the ground. Those puffs of smoke would keep rising, and as the wind picked up they grew thicker and higher, and by that time there'd be snow falling too. Then the horizon would disappear. People caught in it would feel like they were going blind in that suddenly flat white world. There's a name for it: whiteout.

Caught in a whiteout, a man loses all perspective, all sense of direction. East, west, up, down—it's all the same. Disoriented, he will start to veer toward one side or the other and begin to walk in a circle. He might struggle on through the drifting snow for a mile, maybe two miles, before he ends up back where he started. At first his toes and fingers will sting, but then the stinging stops. Soon he can't feel anything. His extremities are numb, the eyelashes freeze together and hypothermia sets in. At that point he has begun to freeze to death, a process that takes just a few more hours to complete.

The first major blizzard lasted two days and two nights, and killed a man who had gone out to cut wood and had become lost in the storm, disoriented, wandering in circles, possibly only feet from his own house or barn. After the storm, the police came by looking for him, but they hadn't much hope to offer his wife and children, who were still waiting, huddled together back in their little house. (He would be found in the spring, not far from his house, with his ax still in his hand.) Now Mamie understood beyond any doubt that this prairie would not suffer fools or weaklings, but would cull them as surely as it culled the weak or the unwary among the wild animals who shared her new home.

They were short of everything, including fuel, and after that first blizzard Mamie would sit in her kitchen during the late afternoon, watching the light fade. *It's only four o'clock. Why is it getting dark so early?* That's when she began lighting a coal-oil lamp in the window, leaving it burning all night long, from early dusk until dawn. In their small stove they were using lignite coal, which was cheap from a local source, for there was coal almost under their feet, and in some places it could be dug out of the ground with a shovel and carried home in a basket. They had a small wood pile too, mostly scraps from the poles they'd used in the house and barn, but it was still too green to burn well, and there wasn't much of it in any case.

One night at the end of November a bad storm blew up, and

after the children had been put to bed and Mamie was alone with her worries, she was startled by a noise outside the door. Half terrified, hardly daring to hope, she waited, holding her breath. Then the door burst open, and there was Ernest, snow-covered, frostbitten but blessedly alive.

Later, after the children had been hugged and a few adventures had been related, and the two older boys had helped him put the horses away and gone back to bed strangely subdued, the howling storm seemed to change its tune, for now it was like music to Mamie's ears. Winter prairie music, singing its own song outside her little doby house that was no longer a lonesome, frightening place, but suddenly cozy with the good smell of fresh coffee and her husband sitting near her with his feet on the oven door, and her children all safe in their beds. She asked Ernest how he'd found his way home in the dark and the storm, and he told her he nearly hadn't, that he'd almost missed the house, but he'd seen the light in the window. For the first time in more than a month, Mamie felt joyful and hopeful because everything was all right again.

And later, when she had blown out the light and they were lying close and warm in their own bed? That's when I think he told her about the horses, whispering the bad news into her ear. How he'd only managed to bring three of them home and how awful he'd felt when the best one of all had sickened, and there was nothing he could do—it just died.

At that time, the market for draft horses was booming. The devastating winter of 1906–07 had all but finished the big cattle ranches in the district. Early blizzards and the longest, hardest winter anybody on the prairies had ever seen killed off more than half the cattle in southern Saskatchewan; some of the old-timers insist it was closer to 70 percent. Although cattle died like flies that winter, and their bloated carcasses fouled the creeks and turned the air putrid the following spring, somehow the horses survived the cruel weather. That winter had ended what was left of the ranching monopoly in the south, and the incoming farmers needed draft horses to break up the prairie. There was money in heavy horses, big money in a good stud, but the best horse in the world wasn't worth spit if it was dead.

This is the story I heard at the sewing machine, while my mother and Mamie made bib aprons. That night, Ernest admitted to her that the horse he'd lost was worth more than everything he'd earned while he'd been away.

It about broke his heart, she would say, each time the story unfolded. Dutifully on cue, my mother would reply, *It didn't make you feel terrific either* or *That must have been awful,* and they'd both look solemn while Mamie rocked back and forth in the squeaky rocker and Mom stepped on the treadle and ran another seam.

It wouldn't be much of a Christmas, Ernest told Mamie, but he supposed they'd get through the winter all right. After he fell asleep, and Mamie had given thanks for his safe return, was it any wonder if she cried a bucketful of tears into her pillow?

By that time the buffalo were long gone from the prairies. Nor were there many of the white-tailed deer or pronghorn antelope that would one day make a comeback. Fortunately, the two older boys were good shots, and the disease called tularemia had not yet infected the rabbit population, so Mamie relied on rabbits and prairie chickens for meat to feed her family through the winter.

She was a frugal housekeeper, but she intended to splash out just once that year: she was fattening a goose—the big gander—especially for Christmas. There wouldn't be any gifts and no Christmas tree, but at least she could give them a Christmas dinner. She'd even hoarded an onion for the stuffing, and every now and then when she went into the root cellar, she'd have a look at that onion, just to be sure it was okay and not rotting or freezing or getting chewed by mice. (She told me about the onion, and one of the uncles remembered it too, as though it had been some luscious, exotic fruit.)

There were still a lot of eagles around southern Saskatchewan in those days, and it was a evidently a large golden eagle that drew a bead on Mamie's Christmas goose, who was strutting around the yard, soaking up the winter sunshine as though he owned the place. Mamie must have been working outside when she heard the goose honking furiously, then squawking in distress, because the uncle who told me the story (he was fourteen at the time it happened) insists that she almost managed to save the bird. "She came around the corner of the house swinging her broom, and if that eagle hadn't let go of the goose she'd have beat it to a pulp, she was that mad."

The eagle retreated under Mamie's fury, but not before it had mortally wounded the gander, ripping a huge gash in the breast. Once again, the prairie had played one of its endless tricks. A clear day, a golden eagle, and it was good-bye goose. For Christmas they had rabbit potpie eked out with potatoes and an onion. Mamie was beginning to understand why some people were already calling this prairie "next year country."

The uncle who shot that particular rabbit never forgot his first Canadian Christmas dinner. More than once he described to me how delicious his mother's potpie had been, maintaining with true Dickensian fervor that no dish he had tasted before nor since could have touched that Christmas rabbit for its flavor, its tenderness and its generally sumptuous perfection.

The fact that anyone had a single charitable memory of that first long, meager winter, with seven people living in such a confined space, is either a testimony to a child's faith or to the strength of Mamie's family. Burdened with the isolation, the poverty and the utter hopelessness of their situation, many families broke under the strain, and tragedy struck with regularity. Men ran away or drank too much or brutalized their wives and children or went mad or died of a broken heart or killed themselves or simply disappeared.

Oddly enough, the women seemed to hang on. They stayed because of the children or because they saw no other option, or maybe they hadn't enough energy left to care.

Only a child could have failed to be terrified by the infinite possibilities for disaster that lived with them during that first winter on the south Saskatchewan prairies.

Recipe from the Cash Book

Rabbit Pot Pie

Skin out the rabbit and cut in pieces as for frying. Boil with a little salt until meat comes away from the bones. Pick out the bones, and put meat in a tin basin with a cut up onion. Season the juice with a little pepper, thicken with browned flour, add a lump of butter. Cover with rich biscuit dough and bake an hour, but do not have too hot an oven for fear of scorching.

Biscuit Dough

Bowl full of milk.

About 3 tbsp sour cream.

Pinch soda maybe. Leave awhile on warming oven.

Stir in 1 tbsp soda, 1 tsp salt, flour to kneed nicely.

CHAPTER 9

The Pursuit of Loneliness

Be you the new light 'crost the valley yonder?
Ye don't know what a comfort they've been to
me this winter.

—ANONYMOUS

*F*OR WOMEN, THE NEW FRONTIER
brought an isolation that was decreed by distance, poor transportation and climate, but all three reasons put together didn't make up
for the solitary nature of their lives. There is a difference between
being alone and being lonely. Any stranger in a big city can attest to
that. So can anyone who's ever been marooned at a cocktail party, the
only outsider in a room full of other people's friends. Being alone
can be constructive, even satisfying, and if nothing else, it's good dis-
cipline. On the other hand, prolonged loneliness will eat away at a
woman's spirit and have her talking to herself and crying for no reason, and eventually it will break her heart, whether she's in a big city
or on an empty frontier.

The prairies were hard on immigrant women like Mamie, but
she had the distinct advantage of being able to speak English. Some
of her neighbors, the ones she referred to as Galicians, knew almost
none. How much worse it must have been for them, so far from anything familiar or comforting, isolated even from ordinary conversa-

tions with other women because they couldn't speak English. Their homesickness must have been terrible.

Mamie was five miles from her nearest neighbor and even farther from Wood Mountain Post, where there was a store, a post office and a police detachment to provide at least the illusion of a cosmopolitan world—newspapers, bolts of cloth, food in labeled cans, conversation that did not revolve around the same old domestic trivia. The nearest large hospital was in Moose Jaw, one hundred miles away, and the nearest doctor was sixty miles away, but he might as well have been on the moon.

She was alone at critical times. She had three of her nine children with no one but her husband to help her through labor and delivery, and during one December night in 1918, when the entire district was gripped with the influenza epidemic that took fifty thousand Canadian lives, she came close to death while my mother was being born.

"We were lucky," Ken recalls. "Some of us had the flu, but mildly, and no loss of life in our house, even though Dad was out every day, helping. . . ."

The following year Ken developed quinsy, and for three months Mamie nursed the child, staying up nights, then putting in a full day's work until she was exhausted.

Ken: "Then Pearl got sick. I guess she had convulsions during the night. For a while she couldn't talk, couldn't walk—she was shaking all over. We didn't know what was wrong."

Mamie was afraid Pearl would die and kept her alive by sheer force of will. She would not lose another child, not if she could help it. They had a name for my mother's sickness—it was called St. Vitas Dance, for reasons I've never been able to determine. (In later years she would develop multiple sclerosis, and although no medical connection was established at the time, I've always wondered if that mysterious childhood illness had anything to do with it.)

Ken: "I remember when Dot got a sore throat that turned into abscessed tonsils. They bundled her up and took her by sleigh with four horses, all the way to Assiniboia. The doctor operated on her right in his house. It was Pop who held the ether." What did Mamie do, I wondered to myself, while her child was having surgery on a kitchen table, and as though he'd read my mind Ken said, "I guess she was praying."

Apart from the other emotions that would attend such an existence, it must have been a lonely way for a woman to live. Not lonely for the sound of another human voice, for with her husband and all her children there'd have been plenty of voices; but for the thoughtful, sympathetic ear of a friend, another woman of her own age and experience to talk to, worry with, laugh with. That's what was missing.

It was probably a good thing that Mamie was religious, and her relationship with her God was never closer than when she was walking alone over the prairie. *God sees the little sparrow fall*, she taught me to sing. *It meets his tender view. . . .* Mamie loved to sing. She knew every hymn in the gospel repertoire and taught most of them to me. In later years I'd get out of practicing my assigned piano lesson by banging out gospel hymns on the piano. As long as I kept the hymns coming, nobody requested scales, and she and Pearl would warble the soprano to "Shall We Gather at the River" while I'd make up the alto and my Dad would come in on the tenor if he was available.

For Mamie the prairie was a living, breathing allegory that constantly renewed her faith and proved once and for all that the hand of the Almighty was on the cosmos. As she grew old she often pointed this out to me. How else to explain a hawk riding the wind in complete safety or a flower turning its face toward the sun? Even the coyote scavenging for carrion didn't hunt on his own. He had divine help, she assured me, though as a poor dumb animal, of course, he wouldn't know it.

To everything there is a season, she'd quote, *and a time for every purpose under heaven.* After the Song of Ruth, this passage from Ecclesiastes was her favorite piece of scripture. She would recite it to me in lieu of a bedtime story, but I found it dull, so I tried to spice up those moments with my own take on season and purpose. Do potato bugs and cutworms have a purpose, I'd ask, by way of provoking conversation as long as possible, the only other option being sleep. Do aphids have a purpose too? What about grasshoppers? I knew she hated hoppers, crop-eating thieves she called them, but according to her God must have had some purpose in mind even for them, even if it was only to keep humans from getting too big for their britches.

How about snakes, Gram?

Touché. She didn't defend snakes. They had their uses in the natural order of things, against mice and other such grain-eating pests, but they gave her the heebie-jeebies and their record was not entirely unblemished. In the Garden of Eden it had been a pesky snake that got Eve into trouble and landed the rest of us womenfolk right smack in hot water, where we'd been ever since. Sometimes it just seemed as though the world was going to the dogs. . . . She'd say this bit about the dogs softly, thoughtfully, and I remember puzzling over that particular metaphor. Dogs, after all, were among our favorite companions. But she wasn't afraid of any of it. Bugs, snakes, coyotes, wind, isolation—she learned to take it in her stride, even if she didn't like it. The world could go to the dogs and she could handle it.

Notes from the Cash Book

Distance from here.
Moose Jaw, 110 mi. n
Wood Mt Post, 6 mi. n
Limerick, 35 mi. n

US line, 16 mi. s
Willow Bunch, 30 mi. e
Killdeer, 6 mi. e
Maple Crik—a long way

Mamie's Children

CHAPTER 1

In Mamie's Gardens

MAMIE HAD TWO GARDENS, AND she loved them equally. One was the grassland itself, the whole blooming prairie, rolling out its scented carpet of flowers and shrubs from early spring until fall, and in any year with enough rain it was, and still is, a wonderful sight to behold. The other was the spot she worked so hard to tame, her private garden where she planted carefully hoarded seeds, coaxing an abundance of food and flower from the reluctant earth.

The first prairie flower of the year is the crocus, which we were taught to call pasqueflowers on science exams. Mamie, looking out the south window from the boys' room one April morning, would have seen a cloud of them in her meadow, and her eyes must have rejoiced in their color. In the prairie landscape, a wild crocus is the color of spring itself, a shade so delicate that it falls somewhere between a field of flax in bloom and a lilac. The fuzzy stem is short and silver-gray, and sometimes I've noticed a faint sheen on the outside of the petals, neither silver nor green, but far more delicate, as though the flower had brushed against a wolf willow before the paint was dry.

Next would come the dandelion, despised by city folk, but one of Mamie's useful plants because of its bitter, vitamin-rich leaves, which nobody especially liked, but lots of people ate anyway, as they were such a tonic after a long winter. Cook them like beet greens, with a small onion, a discreet blob of bacon fat and a dribble of vinegar at the last minute; so says the Cash Book. Speck of salt, pinch of pepper, and they're done. Serve 'em up with pot likker if you're so inclined. Mamie always served her greens swimming in the cooking juices because the two older boys preferred them that way, and then they'd mop up the residual juices with bread and smack their lips loudly, which is why my mother steadfastly drained her vegetables before they came to the table. If a single errant drop of juice clung to her spinach before she poured on the melted butter, she'd blot it away, recalling out loud how she'd learned to hate vegetables that were undrained, "Slopping around the bowl in that darned soup, just because Roly and Roy liked them that way."

Notes from the Cash Book
Dandelion Greens, Mrs. Hicks
Dig up plants early, when buds are tight. Wash in three waters until clean. Trim off roots. Put in salted water over a good fire. Cut in small onion. When it boils, add pinch soda. When cooked, add bacon grease and some vinegar for flavor. Roots can be roasted and ground for a nice drink in place of coffee.

If Mamie had been anything but a teetotaler, she might have made another specialty of the prairie springtime: dandelion wine, a yellow, resinous-tasting concoction brewed from dandelion blossoms. She could have dispensed it by the thimbleful to grateful sopranos during choir practice, and they would have obtained a pleasant buzz and likely asked for seconds. And then, how they'd have made the rafters ring.

On a summer day in 1996, riding horseback through the old pasture near where Mamie and Ernest's doby house stood, I'm too late for crocuses and dandelions, too early for goldenrod or bright yellow tansy with its dark, ferny leaves, a flower that Mamie liked in fall bouquets with purple asters. Instead, from the considerable height of Slicker's back, I have an aerial view of Mamie's wild garden in midsummer, when the wildflowers are at their best and most abundant.

Pink is everywhere, in every shade—pink yarrow, pink clover, the pink prairie rose with a heady perfume that lasts a long time. In the upturned faces of black-eyed susans are dark centers like velvet buttons fringed with golden-orange petals. Over there, the blaze of an orange lily with chocolate-brown stamens, the ones Mamie called tiger lilies. Cezanne, the man who painted oranges, would have loved these lilies.

A wild tiger lily is an independent flower, fending for itself under the hot sun and the foraging of animals. Mamie taught me not to pick them because the shock of being yanked from their chosen spot is too much to bear and they would wilt before we could get them home and into a fruit jar of water.

"Too pretty for their own good," she told me sternly, as though the lily had somehow shown weakness of character by being so drop-dead gorgeous. I knew it was another version of *Handsome is as handsome does.*

Not all wildflowers are so delicate as the orange lilies. On this midsummer day Mamie could have picked an entire field of white oxeye daisies, but she wouldn't have bothered with them because they smelled bad, just like a house cat's litter box, she'd say.

Bluebells and queen anne's lace were pickable. So were yellow cowslips and purple buffalo bean, and the lacy bunches of baby's breath that could be hung upside down to dry. If she wanted to make a more dramatic statement with a summer bouquet, she used tall purple spikes of sweet rocket or the even taller wild parsnip. From early spring until fall, there was the silver-gray of wolf willow and the butter-colored blossoms of a low-growing shrub she called cinquefoil, pronouncing it *sink-way-foyl.*

On the west side of the doby house, in a spot that caught the full sun from the morning until night, was Mamie's other garden—a half-acre of vegetables. Walking the old homestead on another day this summer, in what was once her backyard, I step on mint plants so potent that their scent rises cool and fresh in the heat of the day, and I can taste the lemonade she and Pearl taught me to make with real lemons, a pale straw color, with pieces of rind in the pitcher, a handful of mint squashed into the bottom, and the glasses beading up in the heat.

Like Mamie, this garden is a survivor. Her rhubarb and horse-radish are still thriving, both plants having seeded themselves over and over, hither and yon around the farmstead until they're closer now to their wild state, the way they were when they arrived in North American soil, planted by the hand of some lonely Central European woman, far from her original home in the Caucasus. I never loved horseradish, still don't, but Mamie cherished the stuff.

"Your grandmother was quite famous for her beet and horse-radish relish, you know," a local woman tells me. She thinks I'm writing a cookbook, or at least I should be. She can't imagine why I'm interested in the history of this place anyway; she's lived here all her life and nothing's ever happened yet that surprised her, except maybe the excellence of Mamie's beet relish.

"I think she put cabbage in it too. It was the best beet relish I ever tasted. Best in the whole district, I guess. Some folks put in too much horseradish. Whooeey, it'd be strong enough to make your eyes water. Melt the enamel clear off your teeth. But she always got it just right somehow."

Notes from the Cash Book
Beet Horseradish Relish
1 gallon cooked beets, chopped fine
1 gallon green cabbage, chopped
½ gallon vinegar mixed with a little water
1 teacup grated horseradish
6 teacups sugar
2 spoons ground allspice
4 spoons salt
Mix well with wooden spoon. Leave overnight. Bottle.

Mamie transplanted her saskatoon and chokecherry bushes from a neighboring coulee. Walking the land, I stumble on one, its creamy blossoms wobbling under the weight of various bees, half drunk with pleasure. Later in the summer, the bushes will be weighted down with fruit, the chokecherries hanging in glossy, near-black bunches, the saskatoons in fat, dusky clumps, swollen with juice, bigger and bluer than the chokecherries. Sweeter too. I wonder if they're the same bushes Uncle Roly told me about, a few years before he died.

"I remember her hitching old Johnny to the stoneboat, loading the younger children on it, and driving down the coulee to get fruit bushes. She'd dig them up and bring them back to our own garden. Mother could make anything grow. Oh, she'd make chokecherry jelly, chokecherry syrup, saskatoon pie."

AT FIRST THE GARDEN had no shelter at all from the ever-present wind that blew high and hot all summer long. It was a strange, lonely wind, and often she heard the high keening, the wailing in the sky

during the first treeless years, when there wasn't so much as a bending branch to tell which way it was blowing before she stepped into
it and felt its hot breath on her head, pushing her along as she headed for the garden.

Her skin dried up in the heat, wrinkled early, turned leathery,
the color of a walnut. The photo album shows Mamie at forty-two
with white hair, weathered face, looking like she was sixty. The
relentless sun and wind turned her hair brittle and dry as straw. Lips
and fingers cracked, eyes were gritty and sore because the wind was
her constant companion in those early years.

Notes from the Cash Book
Smoothing Lotion
*Mix together 1 teacup rosewater, 1/2 teacup glycerin, 1 ounce white wax, good
pinch borax, a little olive oil. Melt together over slow fire. Stir. Bottle.*

After a couple of treeless seasons Mamie decided to do something about the wind. That's when she dug up the wild fruit bushes
and transplanted them to offer a bit of a windbreak for her vegetable
garden. At first there was plenty of water in the slough, so the wild
saplings grew bushy, and as the years passed, they produced great
quantities of fruit. Later, when the rains stopped coming and the
slough got low and then dried up altogether, she carried water from
the well and lavished on her garden every drop of dishwater and
washwater that was used in the house. By 1996, the slough is gone
again, dry as a bone even in the wet year that I returned. Maybe it
never found its way back after the thirties.

Eventually, Mamie ordered gooseberries and red currant bushes
from the agricultural experimental station at Indian Head, along with
hundreds of saplings: cottonwood poplar, Manitoba maple, silverleaf
willow, all good prairie trees because their root systems go so deep,

and even in dry years they manage to find enough moisture to survive. She planted them in a double row all around the yard, where her dream house would one day stand, and beyond that to the far side of the barn, until she had a formidable number of trees sheltering her from the wind that sang perpetually through their branches. As with the smaller fruit trees, she watered these by hand. Today, from the gravel road that runs past the old homestead, Mamie's trees (or maybe their seedlings) still ride high above the prairie like a dark green island in a pale sea of grass. When the summer wind plays through the leaves, they make a sound like waves on a lake and sometimes like rushing water, which must have been wonderful during the hottest, driest part of the season. When there was rain coming, she'd have heard it first in the wind running through the top branches, closer and closer until the first drops fell, settling the dust and washing the leaves. Even at high noon in the heat of an August day, there would be something of the cool of morning in that double row of trees.

And in the fall, when the poplars turned briefly to bright yellow-gold on a morning after a frost, the watery swishing of leaf against leaf would take on a crisp edge, like the rustle of a stiff taffeta skirt. A few days later, when the leaves were even drier and ready to fall, the sound would have changed again, this time to a faint clicking as they rattled earthward in the wind. It must have been wonderful then to stand among those poplars with the wind lashing the leaves into a blizzard of gold all around her. I'd like to think that on a perfect September day she would have taken a little time for herself, forgetting the washboard and the cooking pots, to walk among those falling leaves, but she never told me about such a moment. When she was old and we walked together *swish swish* through the leaf piles on a warm autumn day, she didn't say, *I remember walking through leaves just like these back in Wood Mountain, when your mother was a little girl. . . .* She would have told me about that, I think, and attached a good story. It was as though she knew, or somehow sensed that even then, time was running out in her prairie Eden.

IT WAS TYPICAL of Mamie's organized personality to grow vegetables in one garden, flowers in another, and in her old age she was fond of reeling off names of flowers I couldn't pronounce, like schizanthus and nierembergia and xeranthemum, which she said were also called paperflowers.

Summer 1996. My Uncle Ken, among the flowers of his West Coast garden, eulogizes Mamie as prairie gardener: "You could say she had a green thumb . . . some people surely said that. But she was more. She was a master gardener. The flowers? They were amazing. Poppies, petunias, baby's breath, sweet william. She had a big garden. Almost a market garden. Every coffee tin had a potted plant in it. Flowers? That woman knew how to grow flowers. . . . You never saw flowers like that."

He stares out the window, watching a bird land on the blazing red rhododendron that is his pride and joy, and in my head I hear Mamie saying, *Like mother, like son.*

Her big garden was more than a pleasure. It was essential to her main job: feeding her family year round. Setting a good table was only possible if she grew an abundant garden, and while the planting and growing seasons were busy, the harvesting was an even bigger job because everything had to be readied for storage. *Putting things up for winter,* she called it. *Putting things by.*

Mamie grew every root vegetable that her well-thumbed seed catalogue offered. Uncle Ken remembers it as being from Stokes, or Burpees, but a woman in Rockglen thinks Mamie got her seeds from the Eaton's catalogue, like everybody else. She was right—among the pages of the Cash Book I find an Eaton's mail order form for farm and garden supplies. She grew cabbage and cauliflower and eventually kohlrabi my uncle thinks, but she never attempted a broccoli plant. Although there were green onions in spring and big paper-skinned granex for storage and even an experimental shallot given to her by a neighbor, she never attempted nor wanted garlic in her garden, associating it with the mysteriously aromatic cooking of the eastern Europeans she referred to as Galicians. Still, she learned to use it sparingly, one clove at a time, in her dill pickles.

She did grow tomatoes, cucumbers and dillweed. In these ways she was a sensualist: the smell of the tomato plant when she pinched out the sucker leaves—that intensely green, faintly dusty and totally tomato smell—was one she loved and pointed out to me on hot July mornings in my mother's small vegetable patch, long after she had left her own massive garden behind. Sometimes she'd pick dillweed and crush it between her fingers. "Sniff," she'd say, sticking a crumpled dill frond under my nose. "Good? That's why the pickles taste the way they do."

There were garden chores that she assigned to others, like carrot pulling and potato digging, but Mamie looked after everything else: weeding, watering, thinning, mulching. Daily she'd measure the height of pole beans and corn with her eyes, matching today's reality against yesterday's memory, rejoicing in growth spurts of squash or cabbage, worrying over the stunted or diseased plant as she might have worried over a farm animal that refused to thrive. The garden was her territory, and she didn't much care for intruders. Of course all of this was before the dry years, when the clouds turned into dust, and the rain didn't come at all, and nothing good happened for a long, long time.

Found Objects

Along with the Cash Book, I inherited Mamie's Bible with its onionskin pages and ragged leather cover. For years, whenever I opened it, pressed flowers would come fluttering out. Pansies and nasturtiums seemed to be her favorite candidates for pressing, but there were also leaves. Some were wild—wolf willow and sage—and still faintly scented. Some I recognized as houseplants. And there was one that I was certain came from a grapevine, though where she would have found it is anybody's guess.

The Family Album

Uncle Ken at nine, hair slicked back, eyes squinting shut against the sun, wearing his best Sunday suit, the one with short pants, with a big white Peter Pan collar. He's holding a fistful of flowers.

My mother at three or four, standing by the mud house, knee-deep in petunias. The window behind her is stuffed with houseplants and more foliage billows from a low window box, where Mamie grew kitchen herbs.

The two elder brothers, Roly and Roy, posing by the door before leaving for a picnic, hatbands festooned with huge double poppies.

Notes from the Cash Book

GARDEN, 1915:

April 10, start in house—petunias, pansies, tomatoes, cabbage. Plant sweet peas outside.

May 24, 6 rows peas, 6 rows string beans, 4 rows beets, 8 rows carrots, 40 hills potatoes, 8 rows corn, 10 hills cucumbers, 8 hills citron.

June 4, set out 37 cabbage plants, 24 tomato plants.

FLOWER GARDEN, 1918:

Candytuft, bluebottle, baby's breath, china asters, four o'clocks

Rose mallow and hollyhock (Mrs. Hill),

Red poppies double (Mrs. Oakes).

CHAPTER 2

The
Cash Book

*M*AMIE'S CASH BOOK WAS FULL OF
recipes. The recipes were a legacy of other women, secrets of flavor
and texture, these vital formulae that were passed from friend to
friend, mother to daughter, one generation of women to another.
For many of them, the daily business of cooking was far more than
an unavoidable chore. It was part science, part art, possibly the most
useful art of all, and there was considerable personal satisfaction in
setting a good table and in growing, harvesting and storing what
went on it.

Mamie's Cash Book contained her recipe for her most memorable dish—chicken soup with fresh noodles. Years and years later in
a kitchen in Bologna, Italy, I watched an Italian chef make noodles
exactly the way Mamie had eventually taught me to make them back
in Saskatchewan. The chef chattered away while she made a cone of
flour on the breadboard, but it was Mamie's voice I heard, talking to
my nine-year-old self.

Start with a good pile of flour, she'd tell me. *Thump the middle with your elbow to make a hole, just like that volcano in your book. See? Now break in some eggs.*

Mamie and the Italian would have agreed on the next step. It was important to break the yolks with your fingers and mix the eggs into the flour, moving fast but lightly and always in the same clockwise direction so the dough wouldn't be tough. When it reached the right consistency, it was rolled as thin as possible, floured generously and rolled up like a rug. It was then cut into strips, picked up and tossed in the air to get rid of excess flour.

Remembering all this, I would foolishly volunteer in the Italian chef's class. I hadn't made noodles since Mamie died, but who could forget such a simple thing? And while rolling the dough I got a wrinkle and tried to hide it by rolling over it, and got caught. The famous chef gently berated me for being so clumsy. *Is a simple thing, no? But simple isn't easy.*

Mamie could not have said it better. Simple wasn't easy, but it was life. Men might run the farm that produced the grain and livestock—and when called upon, the women would work beside them—but the planting, growing, gathering, cooking and preserving of enormous gardens, the laying of the table, the baking and cooking and serving forth of the feast, and the cleaning up afterward were women's work. Simple things, but not easy.

The rewards were tangible, and like gardening, cooking had a definite sensual quality. Most women of Mamie's day would have been scandalized if they been described as sensualists, yet nobody knew better than a farm woman the intense pleasure to be found in the smell of rising bread or the little flutter somewhere behind her ribs when the first lettuce made its appearance as a faint green line across the garden on a spring morning, or the deep satisfaction of putting the lid on the last of 120 sealers of wild plum jam.

The careful hoarding of sealers, the swapping of recipes and the dozens and dozens of church and community cookbooks produced on the prairies at that time and for years to come attest to the art and science of the prairie woman in her kitchen.

No prairie farmhouse parlor, no matter how tarted up with stiff Eaton's furniture and starchy lace curtains, was ever as important as the kitchen. The kitchen was both heart and nerve center of the rural home, the room you entered cold and left warm, entered hungry and left well-fed, ready to take another run at the world outside. It was the room in which conversation took place, where children did homework by the light of a coal-oil lamp, where a couple sat late over a last cup of tea, making plans, solving problems, talking of this or that, the minutia of their days and years.

Though men might come and go, the kitchen was a woman's room. It was the room where news and special knowledge were passed among women, where stories were told, feminine mysteries were explored and secrets exchanged. There was always good talk in the kitchen among the women washing dishes after Sunday dinner while the men were elsewhere, digesting. If by accident or design a man should wander in, he was recognized as an intruder. Inquiries would be made in a carefully teasing manner—*Oh look, here's George to do the dishes*—and George would sheepishly disappear, and everybody would be glad when he did, so the womantalk could resume.

Like all the ordinary women who ever set foot on the prairies, most of Mamie's working day was spent in that room. When she moved in with us, she and my mother continued to spend their days in the kitchen, and it was there, among the pots and pans and the smell of rising bread and roasting meat, that the roots of our family tree seemed longest and strongest, for there the best stories were told over and over again.

Long after Mamie's death, my uncles told their own stories. They remembered her as the finest cook ever to grace a dinner table and loved to reminisce about her baking powder biscuits and the six-teen giant loaves of sourdough bread she would produce twice a week, winter and summer, from her wood burning cookstove.

My, but Mom was a wonderful cook, Uncle Roly would say. *She could make anything taste good. Why, I remember her makin' bread—you never tasted such bread, snow white and light as a feather.*

They reserved their highest praise for her Sunday dinners, when the current preacher and assorted religious itinerants and hangers-on usually had their feet under her table, and Mamie would have once again killed some fatted calf or goose in their honor.

Her daughters remembered Mamie's culinary skills in a some-what dimmer light, and having spent years with her in the kitchen, I can honestly recall only two dishes at which she excelled: chicken soup with fat noodles and fried cabbage with vinegar. Plain food, by any measure. I loved both dishes and would love them still if only Mamie were around to cook them because I never quite learned her secrets.

Notes from the Cash Book
Chicken Noodle Soup
1 fowl
1 onion
1 carrot cut up
1 spoon salt
some pepper
Cover fowl with water and set over a slow fire until meat falls off bones. Drop in the noodles and cook until tender.

Make noodles with 2 eggs and flour for a stiff dough. Roll thin as you can. Let dry awhile. Dust with flour. Roll up like jelly roll and cut in ribbons.

If the soup was even half as delicious as I remember, with its abundance of broad, pillowy noodles swimming in their aromatic broth, Mamie could have made a fortune with it today, selling it in a square-shouldered jar with a watercolor picture of a chicken on the label. On the other hand, I'd have done almost anything to avoid eating her bean soup, which was sludgy and bland, and seemed to lodge itself somewhere between my teeth and tongue in a most unpleasant way. The only saving grace for bean soup was to eat it with a slab of lavishly buttered bread and a chunk of sweet Spanish onion. Escoffier she wasn't.

Of all her daughters—Pearl, Dot, Myrtle and Nell—I remember that Myrtle and my mother were both superb cooks, proudly competitive of their skills, which were admittedly greater than Mamie's, though there's no doubt she did all that she could with what she had. Dot also was a good cook, but we saw less of her so my sampling opportunities were minimal. Nell could have cooked if she'd wanted to, just as she could have climbed a mountain, shot a tiger or built her own log cabin. She was a capable woman in every way, but cooking was never her priority. On the other hand, she knew how to deal with bull snakes: "If you meet one on a path, you just grab it by the tail and give it a good snap—break its back. It won't bother you again," she told me, laughing, so one half of me believed her and the other half just hoped I never met one in case I had to find out.

While it's true that Mamie might not have invented Cordon Bleu, she shone as a stove-top chemist, a concocter of remedies, and viewed her kitchen as a sort of laboratory. In another life she would have made a good pharmacist, but as it was she did only what was necessary. At least half the recipes recorded in her Cash Book were for essential but inedible potions—fly spray, soap made of ashes and lard, a glycerin and rosewater skin softener, linseed cough mixture (also recommended for urinary infections), whitewash, water-based paint for wooden floors and vegetable dyes from beets or spinach or onionskins. If necessity inspired these useful domestic concoctions, sheer desperation was behind the medicinals that also came from her kitchen. Operating on the theory that if her potion didn't exactly cure her patients neither would it kill them, she had a remedy for almost every illness, including rheumatism and the common cold (an essence of linseed oil, vinegar, raisins, aniseed and honey). *For stiff joints, put a fresh-dug potato in your pocket. Carry it always to keep supple.* My own father did this for years, carrying the same small potato around until it was flat and shiny with age, and hard as a rock. He's spry at eighty-seven.

Mamie had a remedy for whooping cough, the flu and something known only as *spells*, which probably covered anything from fainting to senility and dementia. While her medicines have an eccentric ring to them now and might well have had the city-dwelling physicians of her day falling off their chairs laughing, they were desperate remedies at a time when whooping cough could snuff out a child's life overnight, and influenza could and did wipe out whole families. The influenza epidemic of 1918, a strain of Spanish flu, killed more than fifty-thousand Canadians and had an odd predilection for young, healthy victims. Her remedies, primitive though they may have been, were all she had.

One recipe in particular—her cure for "spells"—was an oddity in Mamie's repertoire because it contained the demon rum. She was temperance with a capital *T*, a teetotaler who wouldn't have added a drop of hard liquor to a fruitcake if her life depended on it. Yet in the matter of the dreaded spells, a recipe firmly directs the caregiver toward this distinctly alcoholic brew: *Cut up a pound of best raw beefsteak, small. Lay it in a Mason jar. Pour over it a quart of rum or rye whiskey, cover it close, and let it set a day or two.* After that it was to be decanted and doled out by the spoonful.

Recently, while walking Mamie's old pasture, I stumbled across a thick piece of glass, evidently the bottom of a large jar, with part of a serial number and the letters *son* standing out clearly in their heavy Braille way. Running my fingers over the rough letters, I wondered if this might have been her jar of choice for The Recipe.

As a child, I often had bronchitis which would degenerate into something everybody referred to as the croup, an asthmalike condition during which I could barely breathe, and terrified that I was suffocating, I would begin to howl and make it even worse. If Mamie was on one of her visits, her remedy was to dose me with one of the few patent medicines she ever used: electric oil. Along with a sort of all-purpose green salve called Zam Buck and the bottle of sweet-smelling Friar's Balsam, electric oil came from itinerant peddlers, who chugged around the prairie backroads in their rattletrap cars. Once a year or so they'd lug a couple of battered black sample cases into our kitchen, dispensing vanilla and almond extract for cookies, cinnamon and cloves for fruitcakes, mixed spices for pickling and a small selection of pharmaceuticals that covered everything else.

The electric oil wasn't as bad as it sounded, and it beat having the back of my throat swabbed with a turkey feather dipped in kerosene, which Mamie assured us would have done the trick if my mother hadn't intervened (never an easy thing once Mamie was in full sail with a project). Considering the name, I wonder if the oil was somehow derived from electric eels, much as the potent brew the Thai know as fish sauce is squeezed from fermented anchovies after they've been encouraged to rot in the hot sun for several weeks.

Mamie's remedy for severe croup: dribble electric oil generously on a teaspoon of sugar and force the protesting victim to swallow it. Hard as it was to swallow while my swollen throat felt like sandpaper, the fact of Mamie's presence with the magic elixir in hand had a calming effect on both me and my mother, who had a tendency to get nursishly brisk at such times, which only increased my terror. But here was Mamie, taking charge, saying, "Pearl, go get a cold cloth for her throat." After all, if I'd really been about to die, would my own grandmother be waltzing around the house in her flannel nightgown with a spoon in one hand and the electric oil bottle in the other? Not a chance. She'd have been standing by my bed in her good black dress, looking solemn and twisting a handkerchief, instead of chirping away about how I should get this down so we could all go back to sleep.

After the electric oil, the cold cloth would be wrapped around my throat while Mamie explained that it would make me breathe better. Oddly, after the initial gasp, it did. By that time my hovering mother would have set up a blanket tent over my bed, and the sweet-smelling concoction called Friar's Balsam would be wafting its aromatic steam my way. The final touch was having the dreaded mustard plaster applied to my chest. I figured it was capable of burning the hide off a rhinoceros, but at least I'd live until morning.

Mamie's curatives weren't exclusively for human consumption, as she was also skilled at bringing sick or injured animals back from the brink. Twice during the years she lived with us I watched her rescue one of my beloved dogs that would almost certainly have died, as the nearest veterinarian was miles away.

The first one was a pup, one the series of fox terrier types I named Spotty. In a matter of hours he'd gone from being playful to listless, and then he'd fallen unconscious, and his stomach ballooned and became rigid. When he stopped breathing I watched in amazement as she pried Spotty's jaw open and blew short, hard breaths into his mouth while giving his small chest a series of firm squeezes. *Look here, Honey. He's comin' around. See? He'll be just fine. Now you run quick and fetch me the electric oil from the medicine cabinet. . . .*

I don't remember the rest of the convalescence, but Spotty

recovered and grew up to become Spot, the terror of the local chicken coops.

The next one was George, a large, friendly collie-type mutt who adopted us and hung around until he became a *de facto* member of the family. George was mostly black, but he had three white socks and a white patch on his tail, as though his mother had shopped around for the right combination. He also had an overabundance of canine charm, and if he'd been a man instead of a dog, I believe he could have lived very well as a gigolo in any number of upscale watering holes. Every spring he'd take off and be gone for days, at which point I'd start to worry, and Mamie would explain that George was just away at a wedding and would be back.

One spring after he'd enjoyed a brief fling with a comely mongrel, he decided to fight the entire local canine population in celebration. Eventually, George turned up in a ditch near our house, gasping his last breath, so my parents made a blanket into a makeshift stretcher and lugged him home, where we all stood around checking his wounds. One eye was swollen shut, an ear was ripped and bloody, he was bruised, bitten, gouged and generally whupped. Possibly because he heard me beginning my death wail, George raised his head a little, gave one mournful groan, flopped back and looked dead.

Mamie hove into view, said, *Hmpf, I've seen worse. Maybe this'll teach the old fool to behave himself,* and sent me for the electric oil. As I recall, it was administered along with a thin gruel of leftover oatmeal porridge, which was his favorite dinner whenever he was in residence. George was back on the road in no time.

Notes from the Cash Book
Paint for Wood Floors
Put 3 qts rainwater and 3 oz glue on stove to dissolve. Add 3 pounds yellow

ochre, or a little burnt umber if a tan shade is wanted. Paint floor. When dry, go over with linseed oil.

Mrs. Demach's Cheap Fly Dip
small teacup of cresol stock dip
1 qt water
1 pint used crankcase oil
Stir well. Wipe on a horse or cow with a rag every day or two.

Linseed Tea for Coughs (Mrs. Hicks)
Boil 1 dessertspoon of linseed in 1 qart rain water until reduced some. Strain. Add a little honey and lemon juice. Give as needed.

Rosewater
Put 1 qt wild rose petals in 1 teacup rainwater. Boil for 10 minutes. Cover and leave several hours. Strain, pressing the petals well.

Summer 1996. Vancouver. Uncle Ken chews thoughtfully on a salmon sandwich, and we have another cup of tea in the china mugs while he mulls over the details of Mamie's life. The old buffalo wallow that in the spring became, briefly, a minuscule pond for Mamie's ducks to paddle around. The names of her horses—Old Frank, Old Johnny, Old Blue. It seemed her horses were all born old. Uncle Ken even remembers her cats.

"I remember she had one big white cat named Ginger. The doby house was infested with mice, and she took the buggy and drove ten miles to get Ginger when he was a kitten, then drove him back ten miles. Looked after him like a baby at first, till he knew the ropes, but he was a quick study. The mice didn't have a hope after he moved in. He had a striped tail, red and white, I guess that's why she called him Ginger. He sure was a great mouser, that cat. . . ."

He recalled her skill as a seamstress and the clothes she concocted from flour sacks when times got tough.

"People at church used to wonder where the Harris girls got

their pretty clothes. Pearl had one dress that was so pretty, everybody asked. They were flour sacks, but Mom fixed them so's you'd never know."

I knew the story by heart because it was one of Mamie's favorites. I'd heard all about her couturier treatment of flour sacks, and the embroidered tea cloths and other fancywork those crafty pioneer women had devised from empty flour and sugar bags. It was another part of the female mythology, told at the sewing machine by Mamie while she and my mother basted the hem of a dress for me to wear to church. My mother didn't say she'd hated the famous flour-sack creation, but I got the idea she was just as happy to be sewing her own daughter a dress without *Purity Flour* stamped across the rear end.

CHAPTER 3

View from a High Window: 1925

*T*HE THING WAS, MAMIE LOVED wide-open spaces. They represented the ultimate freedom and appealed to her sense of adventure. She wanted to be able to see as far as possible in all four directions. That's why, when she sat down to design her first real house on the Wood Mountain homestead, she drew a square, 24x24', two stories high with a gabled roof and an attic.

Upstairs, under each gable, were three tall windows, the middle one being a touch taller than the other two, which gave the window a surprised look, like a slightly lifted eyebrow. From those windows she could scan the entire prairie, at least until her trees grew too tall. What a view it must have been. Downstairs was a living room with ten-foot ceilings, a big kitchen with a separate pantry, and Mamie and Ernest's small bedroom. Down one more flight was the full-sized basement, and local people remember that Mamie had a large summer kitchen down there with a long table, where most meals were prepared and served.

"Not far from the new house we had a deep well fed by an underground spring. It flowed so fast, why you could pump it dry and in half an hour it would be full again. She had a sort of cold room built over the pump for keeping butter, cream, eggs. . . ." Uncle Ken told me this.

The first time I saw Mamie's dream house I was eight years old, and we were visiting my mother's third oldest brother, Leonard. Uncle Len raised cattle, and the idea was to help with the roundup and branding and visit the old homestead so we could tell Mamie all about it, complete with a whole roll of snapshots Mom planned to take with her new Brownie Starflash. I'd heard so much about the house that I expected it to be exactly the way Mamie and my mother remembered it—butter yellow with white trim, the smell of bread baking downstairs in the summer kitchen and the sound of a choir in the living room, practicing "Shall We Gather at the River."

Many of the stories that passed between my mother and Mamie during the years when we all lived together began and ended in Mamie's dream house. As the chief audience for these family tales, I could have walked through that house blindfolded and gone straight to the flour bin, the jar where she kept the gingersnaps, the woodbox behind the stove, the plant stand with the fern on it. I could have found the kittens in the barn loft, where the old white cat hid them. I felt as though I'd been there the day she brought them out for viewing, and I could almost remember hearing the little girl, Pearl, arguing forcefully for keeping all five.

Such was the power of myth and history as told by these two women that the entire fabric of their lives together before my time, and Mamie's before my mother's time, became interwoven with my own brief existence, and it seemed so real in their telling of it that it was as though I'd lived it with them. All their joys and sorrows, told and retold to each other and to me, had become my own. And so I expected, like some latter-day Alice, to be able to walk through a looking glass into those southern hills and that house and be part of it all, like a welcome guest at a family reunion.

When at last we arrived at Mamie's dream house, it wasn't at all what I'd expected. I was disappointed, as only a child can be who hasn't yet learned the social skills of the poker face and the white lie. This was it? An abandoned relic with broken windows, a door hanging by its hinges? Not a scrap of butter-yellow paint anywhere. No flower bed, no big white cat, nothing the way it should have been. The place felt lonely and looked haunted, and I thought it was an ugly old wreck of a house and said so.

Mom didn't take a single picture of Mamie's house with her Brownie Starflash that day, not even one. I still have most of her snapshots from that trip: Mom and Dad on horseback, wearing chaps and ten-gallon hats. My dad holding a calf by a rope at the snubbing post, a cloud of dust rising around him. My little brother playing cowboy in Uncle Len's boots with a Stetson over his ears. Me, overdressed in yellow taffeta, looking sullen. Nothing from the old house.

These journeys backward are never easy and not always wise. For my mother the weed-choked yard and the old house scrubbed bare by the wind could only have been a sadness, whispering of the dead and the dying. A kind of melancholy lies over such places. What was it all for, if this is what it comes to?

After we'd spent what I felt was far too long poking around the yard, we got back in Dad's Ford to drive to my uncle's. As we bumped along the overgrown lane, I saw tears rolling down my mother's face, and because I was still young enough to feel terror when an adult cried, I demanded to know why. My dad told me to just be quiet for once, for goodness sake. Although we visited the Wood Mountain uncle several times after that, as far as I know my mother never again went back to Mamie's dream house.

The old house stood empty for years with the relentless prairie winds howling around it in winter and baking it in summer, and for a long time it seemed destined to one day lose its balance and topple over in the wind, as most old houses eventually do out there, given enough time and prairie weather.

Then one day in 1986, during a freak November snow storm, a kind of miracle happened. A young family named Thomson loaded Mamie's dream house on a flatbed and hauled it down the road to their farm.

Summer 1996. Beth Thomson is a tanned, energetic woman who enjoys the prairie way of life. When I knock at her door, she introduces her children, their various dogs and cats, and a baby Vietnamese pig named Sooey, who is temporarily quartered in the large sun porch they've added since the move. Beth and her husband have painted Mamie's dream house a soft pumpkin color and renovated the inside until even Mamie wouldn't recognize it, at least not until she climbed the narrow wooden stairway, the one Ernest built with his own hands. "They don't even squeak," Beth tells me. She hasn't changed the stairs or the landing at the top.

"I've always been curious about the woman who lived in this house. It wasn't very big, really, and with her large family in those hard times, why would she have designed that big open space at the top of the stairs? It's almost like a balcony. It would have been quite a luxury, especially with those tall windows."

The space at the top of the stairs was really just a good-sized landing, but it was to have been Mamie's special place, a place for a chair, maybe a few books, a place for a woman to dream. The western light would keep it bright until late, and the sunset—well, there'd be no better spot to watch a sunset, except maybe from the back of a horse, up on the north ridge. I doubt if Mamie ever managed to get that chair on the landing or to find time to sit in it, but

I know exactly what she had in mind now that I have my own special place for reading and writing and dreaming, and sometimes doing nothing at all.

In one of those odd quirks of history, long after the local people have forgotten Mamie, they remember her house because of a pair of birds. Two turkey vultures were born in an upstairs closet during its abandoned period. In the summer of 1996, as I go about the district, three or four people ask me if I've heard about the little vultures, and two people produce snapshots of a pair of awkward-looking birds covered with white down, peering at the camera with startled expressions. Beth Thomson took some pictures, but first there was a time of patient waiting.

"We went into the upstairs bedroom, and here was this big bird, apparently dead on the floor. My husband poked at it, and it flew at him. It was the mother bird just trying to keep us away from its nest."

In the nest they found two big eggs, and around the nest the mother-in-waiting had stocked a larder of dead mice and gophers, all stinking to high heaven and rotting to the desired state of tenderness, for a baby vulture takes some weeks to learn to cut its meat. So the mother bird was left to her own devices, and one day somebody checked on the nursery and found the pair of downy vulture chicks, white as snow, opening their ugly little beaks for more meat.

CHAPTER 4

Notes from the Pedestal

SUMMER 1996. WITH UNCLE KEN, Mamie's youngest son. Of the four boys, he was the one I came to know well. He's in his eighties now, the age at which I remember Mamie best, and scattered among the Royal Albert tea mugs on the table in front of us are two albums of family photos—his life.

Himself as a little boy squinting into the camera. Mamie and Ernest looking solemn. Ken's brothers and sisters and their multiplicity of horses and dogs. My mother at four in a white dress, knee-deep in petunias. Sepia-toned memories, brittle with age, fluttering from the pages like dry leaves after a long summer.

"My dad was a dreamer, you know. You might say he was a perpetual pioneer. Always on the move, itching to see across the next valley. Looking for the end of the rainbow, I guess. If he was alive today? Why, he'd be off in China or South America or some other frontier spot, staking out his claim."

As we sift through the pages a couple of tears roll unchecked down his cheeks, especially when I ask about Mamie. The Mamie he remembers wasn't the one I thought I knew so well. My Mamie was the sometimes tender, frequently funny, often cantankerous old woman who sighed a lot, especially in the mornings when she looked out her window onto the broadside of a Pool elevator. How she must have hated that depressing view, she who so loved the open spaces.

For Uncle Ken, Mamie lived on that pedestal western men reserve for "good women," a lofty height on which they seemed determined to maroon their mothers and other women who matter to them—wives, sisters and daughters—invariably referred to in complimentary form as little gals or little ladies, even if they were older than Methuselah's wife and big enough to ballast a small boat. The old western charm tried hard to turn women into a mythic combination of ministering angel and female Valkyrie, who required help to open a door but was expected to fight a fire or break a wild horse if called for.

Contemporary country and western music illustrates and per-petuates the myth of the good woman, a myth that began in Mamie's era and just won't go away. Recently, watching a popular male quar-tet of good ol' boys on a country music talk show, I was perplexed by the names of their two most recent hits: "Trashy Women" and "Mama and Jesus." When questioned by their female interviewer, they were unable to explain the apparent anomaly of loving trashy women by night and worshipping Mama by day, as it were, and when pressed for an explanation, they dissolved into manly snorts and guffaws. While their performance may have looked ridiculous to contemporary women, neither Mamie nor Pearl would have found anything incongruous about it. In their world there were good women, and now and then there were trashy women, and never the twain should meet, please God. But I never heard either of them make reference to a trashy man.

In his day the western cowboy might very well have lived in his saddle, unwashed, untutored, rootless, emerging seasonally from the hills, perhaps to celebrate Christmas with some hospitable family or to spend a night in town getting a haircut and a good meal, topping off the outing with liberal lashings of rye whiskey and a celebrative night among the trashy women in the local whorehouse. Thus fortified, the next morning he could climb on his trusty horse and head back to the hills for another few months.

It was a different story for cowgirls, who had one big impediment to such a freewheeling lifestyle: they were the ones who had the babies. That small but significant difference was both a blessing and a curse then, as it is today, albeit to a lesser extent. For most women of Mamie's era, the birth of a child quickly followed marriage, and the blessed event effectively robbed her of whatever independence she might have had. From that day forward, she would be compelled to rely on her husband, not so much for companionship or affection, though she would have welcomed that, but for financial support of her child and all the children that would follow. If her husband had a loving and generous nature, she was lucky and her life, though hard, would be bearable and in many ways rewarding. If he was a stingy, dictatorial type who regarded his woman as a property—part domestic servant, part sexual convenience—that was her tough luck. Legally, she was a chattel and she should know her place.

If she sought validation, it had to come from within because Mamie's world cared little about women's thoughts and aspirations. What mattered greatly was her capacity for turning a prairie shack into a home, turning her many children into a family unit, and keeping the whole thing up and running by whatever means were necessary.

Without belittling this contribution in any way, for it was unquestionably vital to the developing community of the prairies, it's worth noting that the myth of a woman's place was most often

Ernest with Mamie holding Pearl, who is probably about two.

abetted by the women themselves. Both Mamie and my mother Pearl bought into an unspoken but powerful domestic gospel: *Thy bread shall be light, thy pastry flaky, thy garden mammoth and weed-free, thy children well mannered, no matter what the effort. Thy laundered pillowcases shall be snowy white and shall hang to dry in matching pairs. This above all: Thy underwear shall hang on inside clotheslines only, properly shielded from the lustful eyes of any passing male.*

The prairie woman married early, gave birth often, worked until she dropped, loved everybody, forgave everything, endured all and cried buckets over the sins of her unrepentant menfolk. And when all was said and done, she'd insist with her last breath that she'd had a wonderful life.

Ernest, Mamie, Roly, Roy, Leonard, Kenneth.

Ernest, Mamie, Nell, Dot, Myrtle, Pearl

Notes from the Cash Book, c. 1912

Mother's Best Gift

Bill sent roses, Anne sent a book,

Mother gave them a proud fond look,

But Jim who lives away out west

Sent what Mother thought was best—

A nice long letter, news of folks,

Family memories, family jokes,

He ended it in his usual scrawl,

"I love you Mother," and that was all,

But Jim's present was set apart

To be carried by Mother over her heart.

Mamie was either luckier or more knowledgeable than many of her peers. Unlike those women who had a child every year until their physical bodies and their spirits simply wore out, Mamie had only nine full-term pregnancies and, of these, only one died in childhood. Her children were relatively well spaced, and while it's certain that none of them were planned pregnancies, her last child Pearl, my mother, was the only one she really did not want.

She told me this during an adolescent scrap, when I'd already reduced my mother to tears by being particularly snotty. Ordinarily, Mamie would have told me to hush my sassy mouth, but this time she chose to confide a secret. It seemed trivial at the time though as I grew older I began to see it for what it was—a universal dilemma for women everywhere, throughout time. Pregnancy and birth, which should be joyful, was and still is frequently quite the opposite, burdening the mother physically, emotionally and materially. It seemed that Mamie had been nearly forty-one years old when Pearl was born. Having already raised seven children, she was tired of being everybody's mother and didn't look forward to the financial or physical burden of another baby at her age. But there was a surprise ending, and this was the part she needed me to understand. Pearl, the child she didn't want, in time became her greatest comfort. The moral: dark cloud, silver lining. Her youngest daughter had turned into pure silver in Mamie's eyes and did not deserve my smart-aleck adolescent disdain.

"Where would I be now if it wasn't for your mother? Some days I think she turned out best of the lot. You just remember that, young lady."

Yet even the vocabulary of the western prairies seemed to work against women. The frontier and everything on it had to be conquered. Sod had to be busted, horses had to be broken, dogs and women had to be tamed.

Horsemanship notes from one of the older boys: "We had to break Old Frank. Every time he had a day's rest, we had to break him all over again. I believe he was the most balky horse I ever did see. We tied him each way between two good horses, then he threw himself. We dragged him a ways, and our dog got excited and began to chew the rear end off Old Frank. That was more than he could take. He was broke real good."

Broke was for horses and sod, but *whupped* was the operative term for dogs, women and children. I guess it would have applied one summer day when Pearl, who would have been about six at the time, was playing with a barn cat and didn't come when she was called. The adult brother who went looking for his little sister found her in the barn with the cat, and by this time he was in such an unholy rage that I doubt if he gave a moment's thought to what he would do next. Rather, I see his arm reaching automatically for a length of braided leather they called a blacksnake, a kind of bullwhip used in loading stubborn cattle. It would have been hanging handily low, for he wasn't a tall man, and he'd grown only too accustomed to using it. And none of this excuses his behavior in any way.

Although she told me the story many times as I grew up, my mother never talked about the pain of the beating he gave her. She never said how much it hurt when the whip bit into her bare legs, and I neither asked nor wanted to know. I prefer to think that a six-year-old would go into a kind of shock during such an ordeal, much as adults do when they cut themselves or even break a bone—there are those first few moments when the pain is still waiting to register. But when he threw the screaming child at Mamie, he said something that did register, and my mother's six-year-old brain would keep his words locked there forever. It was a single sentence, and she repeated it every time she told the story until it became a kind of forlorn chant: "That'll learn ya to come when Mommie calls."

Part of the story was about Mamie crying while she washed Pearl's welts, but for some reason she couldn't reprimand the son who had done this to her youngest daughter. That was the part I never understood—that against the fury of her male offspring, Mamie was helpless. I'm almost certain that my grandfather, who was away on one of his many trips when it happened, never heard a word about it.

The story was reserved for my ears only, and by unspoken agreement it was never repeated in front of Mamie, for whom the incident must have been a lasting sorrow and maybe a kind of indictment. It was a two-parter, and Pearl took a grim pleasure in relating the begging-for-forgiveness scene, which came later, a few years after that particular uncle had gotten himself saved at a camp meeting. Part two was where he came to her to ask if she remembered the whupping and fell to his knees, begging for her forgiveness.

"I said I didn't remember," she told me. "I didn't want to give him the satisfaction."

That, too, was part of our female myth, a sort of cautionary tale in reverse that applied to a lot of things. *He shall have no satisfaction.*

There's a caveat to the story. As an adult, my mother wouldn't tolerate violence. She hated the ritual brawling at hockey games and had nothing but disdain for those men who, having drunk more than they could hold at local dances, proceeded to beat each other to a pulp. But if any man had ever raised a hand to either of her children, she'd have flattened him without hesitation. She told me this many times, and I had no reason to doubt her.

Pearl among the petunias at three or four.

After horses, dogs and women, anything left on the frontier could be beaten, trapped, drowned, shot, poisoned or burned, depending on which plant or animal we're talking about. Being harsh, even cruel, was a frontier trait, forgivable and possibly laudable in men, as long as they won the battle. I wonder now if the secret savagery we often showed as children was a function of where we were raised, and if that's why the savage streak was applauded in boys but not in girls. It seemed that when a woman was born with a chronic anger churning in her gut, she would try to control it or hide it, and even if it stayed there, buried deep and making her life miserable, she wasn't likely to let it show, at least not in public. Yet a man with a similar mean streak was allowed to indulge it, even to feed it.

During the long, hot days of summer, when the afternoon lay heavy on our sunburned faces and the little girls I hung out with were bored with dolls, we'd amuse ourselves by collecting potato bugs in a tin can and joyfully setting them alight with a dribble of stolen kerosene. The bugs were actually Colorado potato beetles with hard striped shells, and we laughed when they jumped and sizzled in the flames and then exploded with a sickening little *phhht.* Instinctively, we knew we'd be in big trouble if we got caught enjoying this bug holocaust, although our brothers could and did kill with impunity.

Boys were allowed to kill gophers by whatever cruel method they could devise and then sell their tails, and for a few years they could even collect a municipal bounty of a few cents for gopher tails and crows' feet. Boys had slingshots, and knew how to set snares, and they got their own guns, usually an honest to goodness .22 as soon as they were old enough to site a gopher and pull a trigger. But not girls. Killing for fun or profit wasn't proper for girls.

The day I found a nest of baby sparrows and Mamie caught me drowning them in a tin can, she was shocked and said so. It wasn't the death of three sparrows that mattered to her—sparrows were a nuisance, and prairie women were accustomed to death among the animals. After all, was Mamie not the chief executioner when it came to dispatching a hen for her chicken noodle soup? It was my apparent delight in administering the *coup de grace* that bothered her. She didn't say much, but I knew she was repelled, not by my act, but by the pleasure I apparently took in it. I was ashamed of myself, and to this day, if I close my eyes I can still call up the desperate splashing of those ugly, pinfeathered nestlings.

CHAPTER 5

The

Hell-Raisers

*A*LL FOUR OF MAMIE'S SONS GREW
up to be strong, hard-working men, but peace and tranquillity did-
n't come easily for the two eldest boys, Roy and Roly. They had vio-
lent tempers and were accustomed to indulging them. Although the
beating one of them gave Pearl was the only violence I heard about
in specific detail, it was not an isolated incident, either among the
brothers or in the community.

By the time I knew the two elder uncles, they'd mellowed into
benign old age. As an adult I spent many hours over the teapot with
Uncle Roly while he told and retold his version of the family history.

In an odd turn of events, after their years as angry young men,
they had both become ordained ministers in evangelical faiths, and
my Uncle Roy would eventually design and build several churches in
the western United States. As far as I know, the churches still stand,
a legacy of a long, productive life of Christian service. But in their
early years, there was no getting away from it—the older boys were a
pair of genuine hell-raisers, and Mamie lost a lot of sleep over them.

On the western frontier, a swaggering bully was a less objec-tionable character by far than his opposite number—the milquetoast sissy who unwittingly helped him earn his tough guy reputation. From the genuine gunslingers to the Saturday-night brawlers, bullies demanded and got some measure of respect, even if it was based solely on fear and intimidation of those weaker than themselves. Upheld by laws that turned women into possessions, a man with a short fuse could take his anger out on any unfortunate human or animal that dared to cross him, and if all he did was whip that unlucky creature black and blue or beat it senseless, he'd probably get away with it, at least until he met a bigger bully.

Summer 1996. Early morning on a hot July Saturday. I'm eating waffles with saskatoons and whipped cream in a farm kitchen and talking to the caretaker of the three-day Wood Mountain Stampede and Sports, known in my family mythology as The Rodeo or The Sports. He's been up all night, checking camping permits and main-taining a semblance of order in the tent town that popped up after dark in the surrounding hills, where a big trail ride is now encamped.

"Just like mushrooms," he says, shaking his head in wonderment and piling whipped cream on his fourth waffle. "You'd turn your back a minute, and darned if there wasn't another tent."

"Any serious incidents?" I ask. "Any major problems keeping the peace?"

"Naw. Oh, we had a few fights. A couple of the boys bloodied each other up some, but nothing serious. . . ."

Mamie's eldest boys' habit of bloodying people up some was nothing serious either, at least not by the standards of the time and place. But it burdened Mamie with her most terrible and secret worry: that the eldest son, in one of his rages, might actually kill somebody. She mentioned this private terror only once, after she'd grown safely old and so had they.

When an itinerant preacher arrived in the district and the two older boys declared their intention of going to the camp meetings, Mamie thought her prayers had been answered. She would make the preachers welcome in her home. If there were a few more mouths to feed for Sunday dinners, well, so be it. It was a small price.

1996. A hot July day in the living room of the blue-eyed woman who married Mamie's third son, Leonard, and thus became my Aunt Violet. Today she surrounds herself with those things that matter to her now, photos of her children, grandchildren and great grandchildren. One sepia-toned photograph of her father in profile, sitting on the edge of a sandstone outcrop, his trademark Stetson low over his eyes, his horse leaning over his shoulder.

Another photo: the old corral I remember from my childhood visits. The roundup, calves bawling, pink tongues lolling, big calf eyes rolled back in terror, the smell of burning hair and burning flesh, the almost bloodless castration that I wasn't supposed to see, my dad telling me the branding didn't hurt the calf, he was just bawling for his mother; wanting to believe my dad, knowing it was a lie.

When I was little, I liked Aunt Violet because she was pretty and vivacious, and as comfortable with kids, dogs and horses as she was with adults—a rare quality, in my limited experience, and one I particularly valued in aunts.

When I ask about the preachers, she chooses her words carefully, and it occurs to me that she's probably never discussed this with anybody before and is only telling me now because everybody concerned has been gone for so long and because I have asked her not to whitewash the truth.

"My folks and your grandparents were real good neighbors. If there was sickness or sorrow they went back and forth, and they went to church together in the old Bayard school. I believe that was about the time your people got greatly involved with the preachers who held the camp meetings."

She pauses awhile, probably wondering how much to say, what to leave out.

"There was this one man, Brother So-and-So. I forget his name. He was a raving evangelist, a real hellfire and damnation type. He set up this big tent, and we all went to the meeting. I remember one thing in particular: My mother wore a georgette blouse to church. Real pretty, you know, with long sleeves, but that material was kind of flimsy, and you could see her arms through it. Well now, he preached about it all through the service, condemning her for immodesty, going on about Eve tempting Adam and I don't know what all else."

For a minute she fumes over the memory of Brother So-and-So, whose name she can't remember but whose religious ranting still smarts. She does remember, of course, but out of respect for the dead she won't mention his name, even though it's a matter of public record, and it appears in our family documents more than once. She gets busy shuffling the snapshots on the table, pouring more coffee, hustling back and forth to the kitchen to baste the chicken she's roasting for our supper, but finally she tells her story.

"Mamie's oldest daughter, your Auntie Nell, was a beautiful girl. That preacher had an effect on her. You might say she was taken with him, the way young girls do, you know. . . . Well, she got saved, and he changed her completely. Convinced her she was a real bad sinner. Made her pull all that wonderful black hair back in a tight bun. . . ."

Yes, Nell was a beauty, even when I knew her. I remember the mop of dark hair, the smart clothes, the handbag she sent me from Mexico, the postcards from Africa and Fiji. I remember, on the few occasions when she came back to Saskatchewan to visit us, her habit of throwing her head back when she laughed. So Mamie's eldest daughter, the take-charge world traveler who became my mentor, once upon a time fell under the power.

And now the past is so distant that all I can do is speculate on how it might have happened. How, when Brother So-and-So's traveling salvation show swept northward across the line, it must have been the most exciting thing that had ever happened to her in all of her sixteen years. How could it have been otherwise?

A revival tent is a special place, unlike any other, and there's a sort of holy freedom about a camp meeting that unleashes emotions and encourages bizarre behavior. The smell of oil and dust on the canvas is like incense in the warm air of a summer night, and as the temperature rises in the tent, it becomes a kind of tabernacle, an island of hope in a sinful world.

My aunt remembers: "Those preachers, they'd gather all the evidence into one big pile, and before you knew it you was snowed under by the weight of your own sins and just gasping for breath."

But wait, for the canvas walls billow with the power of love, and in such a place, on such a night, a black sheep can feel enfolded, needed, even cherished by these weeping, laughing, singing, shouting, fellow sinners, who are suddenly so dear and so caring.

Those hot nights in the big tent with the voices raised in the sweet old hymns, *Lamb of God, I come, I come*, there was a charismatic stranger in a black suit striding back and forth, pounding his fist on the Bible, painting hell so vividly that a young girl would feel the flames of eternal damnation licking her ankles.

And here, I think, is how it unfolds:

They're singing *Shall we gather at the river*, and from the direction of the improvised altar a voice booms, *YES Lord! Just HEAR our PRAYER now!*

And the congregation replies in a joyous burst of song, *There is power, power, wonder working power, in the blood, in the blood. . . .*

The American preacher is walking toward her, standing over her, singling her out, resting a big warm hand none too lightly on her shoulder as he pleads for her immortal soul, begs for intercession so that she, SHE, might one day dwell with him in paradise.

COME with me NOW, Sister, come to the AL–tar of JAY–sus!

Amen from the crowd.

Just GIVE me your burden, lay DOWN that sin that's EATIN' your dear heart!

Amen, sister. . . . A–men.

And suddenly a lot of stiff-necked local citizens she's known for a long time are *on their knees,* right down there on the grassy floor of the big revival tent, and they're crying out their testimonies, confessing aloud their most personal sins, sobbing out the sordid details of battles lost with the devil and the demon drink.

The testimonies prove one thing: They're all in this together, this tight little community of lost souls, *Onward Christian soldiers, marching as to war,* because even as their confessions spill out with embarrassing frankness, she hears the voices of her fellow sinners raised in support, like some heavenly cheering section.

I was a sinner, Lord! Drinkin', cheatin', brawlin'.

Amen! from the crowd.

I wasted your gifts, sweet Lord, I squandered them.

Hallelujah! from the crowd.

I sinned against You. . . .

Yes! Praise the Lord forever.

And still the American preacher paces the tent, eyes squished shut, tears running freely now: *Lay ALL your cares on HIM. Do it NOW! Give yer heart to JAY–SUS! TONIGHT, dear Sister. Tomorrow will be too LATE. . . .*

That's it. The clincher. She rises to her feet, this sixteen-year-old country girl in the flour-sack dress, and with the voices urging her on, the crowd swaying around her, crying for her, she walks proudly to the altar.

Hallelujah, Sister, Ha—lay—LOO—ya!

And so on into the night, in the overwrought and overheated manner beloved of traveling evangelists, rainmakers and snake oil salesmen of the day. Strong stuff for a young girl.

"Then one day," says my blue-eyed aunt, "something must have happened. We was all in the kitchen together, all us women, and Nell said she hated that man. All of a sudden like. Told us she couldn't hardly stand to be in the same room with him. From then on, she went right back to being her normal self. I was glad. I wouldn't trust that man as far as I could throw a bull by the tail!"

There's a thoughtful pause now while she chooses her next words carefully, and her gaze, always so direct, wanders out the window to the hills.

"After the camp meetings were all over, the preacher hightailed it back across the line to his wife. . . . Couple of years later, we heard he shot himself."

Mamie, with what she always called her "mother's intuition" (an annoying term that my mother used whenever she smelled a proverbial rat) must have lost a little sleep over Nell's camp meeting conversion and subsequent recanting because a year later she'd scraped up the money to send her eldest daughter to a residential college in Nampa, Idaho, to finish her education.

Meanwhile, a small miracle: Mamie's two eldest sons, the local rowdies, had also fallen under the power and astonished the community by following their sister to the altar, where they had repented and been duly saved. With them, the conversion stuck, and for that the preacher earned Mamie's eternal gratitude.

Sunday dinner took a turn for the better. Nothing exotic, for that would not have been possible, but meticulous planning went into those post-service repasts, and Mamie would allow herself the pleasure of mentally tasting one dish against another, at least until the novelty of holding a kind of perpetual Sunday-at-home banquet began to wear off.

Knowing how she loved food, I can imagine Mamie, pondering dinner: *Let's see now, we had chicken last week, so I'll give them roast pork with gravy. New potatoes. Baby carrots. I'll candy them with a drop of molasses. Green beans with bacon would go down real nice with those carrots, and I'll run up a pan of applesauce in case they don't care for my beet relish. . . . Pie, I guess. Sour cream and raisin, rhubarb and saskatoon, and I could do a couple of carrot pies. . . .*

Sunday after Sunday, Mamie cooked for the preacherfolk and their entourage, and the two older boys became so holy that, as my mother phrased it in later years, they could scarcely get their coats on over their wings or comb their hair for halos. Still, such an extreme change in personality is always unnerving for those who can only stand and watch it happen. When the two brothers erected an altar in Mamie's house and instituted morning and evening prayers for the entire family, and then began reeling off a long-winded grace before every meal, the younger kids stifled their yawns. Tired of being prayed over and preached at by their recently sanctimonious older brothers, they thought wistfully of the hell-raising days.

Meanwhile the preachermen came more often and stayed longer, bringing with them their entourage of wives, children and fellow soul savers.

"Your grandmother worked like a slave," says my aunt. "After a while her house was always full of preachers and their wives, and they'd come and stay a week or two, think nothing of it. It was a real shame, the way those people took advantage of her. Even the ones who didn't sleep over always managed to show up at mealtimes. My mother and dad stopped in one day, and she had a houseful of them as usual, and she invited my folks to stay for a meal. Your grandma was like that, you know, always a hospitable woman. Mama said, 'No thanks, Mrs. Harris—I know enough to eat before I come calling.'"

So, what about you, Mamie? When the voices filled the revival tent with their sweet music and your heart gave that little flutter, did you ever wonder what it would be like to dance, look pretty again, be swept off your feet by a smooth-talking stranger in a black suit? *Yield not to temptation, for yielding is sin. . . .* Didn't you ever wish you could get on Old Frank and gallop away from the drudgery and the sameness, away over the hills, far and maybe forever? *Unto the hills around do I lift up my longing eyes. . . .* But you wouldn't have done that, even if you'd had a chance. *Peace, perfect peace, in this dark world of sin. . . .*

You were no quitter, Mamie. Not then, not ever.

My aunt continues.

"By that time the older boys had got so deeply into this religion thing, they got rambling around to camp meetings, doing nothing at home. One year they bought a big tent so's they could run their own meetings. Great big tent. Paid a terrible price. One night this big wind come up, blew all night long. Wrecked the tent. They lost all that money."

Although she stops short of declaring the wrecked tent the wrath of God, at this point she feels the need to make something crystal clear to me, and the blue eyes are like two searchlights, scanning my face for a shred of doubt because this is important.

"We were all Christian, God-fearing people, you know. My own grandfather was a minister. But good, plain Christianity wasn't enough for that preacher."

And now I know she's still thinking about Brother So-and-So berating her mother for wearing a pretty blouse to church.

"You had to get yourself *saved*, and then they'd be right into your pockets for every cent you had. Your grandfather didn't go for it, and the older boys condemned him, right there in the service. I believe that in the end, your grandmother was walked right down by those religious types."

There was probably not a lot of difference between the Brother So-and-So's, those charismatic men in preacher's clothes who pitched their big tents in the sparsely populated prairies and fleeced whoever they could, and their contemporary clones—a brother Jim Baker, who cooled his heels in an American prison for fraud, or a brother Jimmy Swaggart, whose lurid confessions and crocodile tears held tabloid audiences rapt for weeks. Religion aside, how much does opportunity have to do with motive, I wonder, when there are chickens begging to be plucked?

CHAPTER 6

The Temper
of a Prairie:
1926 – 1935

G RADUALLY, MAMIE'S FAMILY PROS-
pered. In the autumn of 1926 they were farming a full section of their
own land, plus several rented quarters some distance from the home-
place. By virtue of their position on the edge of the coulee, their bot-
tomland had good topsoil, some of which belonged originally to
neighboring farms. Although not every crop was a bumper, Mamie's
family had avoided the pitfalls of the monoculture cereal crops by
diversifying. During the dry years of 1918 to 1922, years that wiped out
straight grain farmers as far west as the foothills of the Rockies, they
had their livestock to fall back on. Of course, the mixed farm was a lot
of work, Mamie said, but when your grain fails, why then you've still
got your beef and milk cows and your laying hens and pigs. As one of
the older uncles recalled, "Everything we did those years seemed to
turn to money. Yessir, God had richly blessed us, He surely had."

The Family Album
Uncle Ken's album is full of horses. Eight-horse teams, four-horse teams, dri-

vers and broncos and garden-variety saddle horses, and Ernest's all-time favorite—
Prince Albert of Pengarth, his prize Belgian stallion.

Albert was a show horse, a ribbon winner at local fairs and even at the big
exhibition in Regina. In the album he stands tall and proud, a great, sleek, muscly
animal that was, he recalls, as gentle as a lamb.

On the next page is a shot of Mamie, standing beside her saddle horse, Old
Ginger. She's dressed for a Sunday ride in a black, ankle-length skirt, a pair of styl-
ishly impractical shoes and a crocheted and tasseled cap that could only be described
as frivolous.

Next page: five kids on a horse, only two of them wearing shoes. The one on
the front, hands on the saddle horn ready for action, is a happy-looking baby, nine
or ten months old, apparently urging the horse to get a move on. That's my mother.

As well as his horses, Ernest had a hundred head of beef cattle
and about that many hogs. Mamie's four boys ran the farm with
their dad, and eventually they had to hire an extra man. Ernest
bought a tractor and then a car, a Model T Ford. Mamie never
learned to drive it, didn't want to drive it anyway, but, oh, how she
enjoyed herself the year they loaded up the younger children and rattled merrily across the line on a holiday, all the way to Arveda,
Wyoming, to visit family.

That was in 1917, the year when Ernest took out two mortgages,
one for $800.00 and a smaller one for $162.66. They were held by
someone named Addison Drake, who may have been a merchant in
a nearby town, possibly somebody dealing in lumber, cars or farm
machinery, the sort of thing a prosperous farmer would feel safe
buying on borrowed money when times were good.

Mamie had the first washing machine in the district because
Ernest believed in laborsaving devices and because he doted on
Mamie and would have bought her the moon if he thought she
needed it. She maintained her poultry flocks, made butter in her bar-

rel churn and kept her huge garden in immaculate condition. Her daughter Nell, away at college, had announced her intention of becoming a nurse, and the other three were safely at home under Mamie's watchful eye. As far as she was concerned, her world was unfolding in the best way any country woman could expect. That's why it was such a shock to her when, as she said on those few occasions when she would talk about it, "Everything just started to go to the dogs."

It was the only explanation she ever gave for what happened to them personally in a time when not just they, but their neighbors and the entire southern prairie, especially the area within Palliser's Triangle, would begin to suffer terribly. If the hard times couldn't be erased from her memory, neither did they make their way into her favorite stories.

It was Uncle Ken who had another explanation, one that became as relentlessly familiar on the prairies as the very wind that blew there day after day: "Dad had become a wealthy farmer, but he went into debt."

Neither Uncle Ken nor anyone else who was there seems to know the specifics, but it's not a hard thing to understand. Ernest simply wanted more land at a time when banks were only too happy to extend credit to successful farmers. It seems that in the end his debts were comparatively small, but, Aunt Violet tells me grimly, by that time, "He was dealing with a loan shark."

Given the circumstances, the shark might have been a small-town banker or the clerk in a mortgage company, stuck with one more loan that shouldn't have gone bad and with little choice but to foreclose. In times of financial crisis on the prairies, such men—clerks, loans officers, managers—often become sharks in the eyes of the farmers their banks purported to serve, as much today as they were then. As it turned out, the shark was in real estate. He lived in another town, but was well known in the district for loaning farmers money against their land and foreclosing when they couldn't pay. Eventually he became wealthy on their losses.

Ernest's personal downfall seems to have begun earlier than most. It began in 1926, when his crops were high and heavy, promising one of the best harvests he'd ever had.

Then came the frost. On the prairies, frost is often an unexpected caller, arriving weeks early some years, pausing at some fields and passing others by, freezing one woman's tomato crop and leaving another's untouched, so the talk in town and on the party lines that day will be of who got hit and who didn't, and those who didn't will thank their lucky stars and vow to cover their gardens tonight.

When the early frost hit their wheat that year, Mamie had predicted it, seen it coming by the smell of the air or the phase of the moon or maybe the red sunrise. She'd covered her tender crops—the tomatoes, the cucumbers and her beloved flowers—shrouded the whole thing in bed sheets and gunnysacks. But you can't cover a wheat field, and when the moon hung high and bright in the sky that night, with not so much as a wisp of cloud cover to protect Ernest's wheat from the coming frost, she knew.

They harvested frozen wheat. It graded so poor it was hardly worth the trouble and expense of threshing. They kept some for seed and sold what they could for what they could get, but it wasn't nearly enough.

The next year, Ernest planted another big wheat crop, only to watch most of it freeze on August 7. That year they harvested seed, but not a bushel to sell, and on December 2 he took out a mortgage for $514.90 at the Bank of Montreal. Three days later, on December 5, he took out a second mortgage for $900.00. This time it was held by three men—Thomas Stinson, John E. Anderson and Alexander

Fulton. None of the names on these aged documents ring any bells with surviving family members, so again I must assume that they were businessmen in another town. By now the debts were mounting, and Ernest was mortgaged in several different directions.

Although 1928 was a dry spring (at Regina the rainfall dropped from 14.5" to less than 6"), there was still some moisture left in the subsoil to kick start the crop, so they tried again. This time they planted all of it to wheat, more than one thousand acres. It should have been a good move, for 1928 was a year in which many of their neighbors, and in fact most of Saskatchewan, would harvest an excellent crop. The average Saskatchewan farmer got more than twenty-three bushels to the acre that year and took home a healthy net cash income of $1,614.

The rain came late, but it came, and so did the hot weather the wheat needed. They didn't think they could miss. Ernest's crop looked good too until he walked through the fields and saw the red pustules along the stems and felt the empty heads and knew there wouldn't be much left because he'd been hit by an outbreak of stem rust. They managed to take a few bushels off a clean field, but even that was a poor grade.

The only bright spot was Uncle Roly's wheat, which was on a higher field on the northeast quarter and was untouched by the rust. It yielded well, so they sold one carload and put the rest in a granary for seed because if the loan shark could be fended off for just a little longer . . . well, there was always next year.

Most of the time, the wind in Wood Mountain country averages somewhere between sixteen and twenty miles an hour, winter and summer, twenty-four hours a day. But it was a perfectly still afternoon when Roly began burning the stubble. When the wind came up from the southeast, it surprised him. In minutes, the sparks from his stubble fire were flying high and wide, jumping the fireguard and landing on the granary. Soon Mamie could smell smoke, and too soon after that came the stench of burning grain.

When a big granary burns, the wheat doesn't turn to ash right away—it smolders and fumes away for days, and smoke hangs in the air, lingers like incense after a funeral, so every breath you take reminds you of your loss. (Mamie remembered the granary fire, years later, when we were awakened in the middle of a winter night because she saw flames dancing on the wall of her bedroom over the railway tracks, and the huge Pool elevator was on fire. Watching my dad and the section men shoveling snow onto our roof because of the sparks, watching our volunteer fire brigade squirting a futile stream into the flames, Mamie held my hand so hard it hurt, and later, in the days and nights while the grain smoldered and stank and the volunteer firemen took turns watching it in case it should start again, she was too quiet.)

On November 19, 1928, the real estate agent placed a lien against Ernest's property. On the documents, much of the writing, including the amount, is no longer legible.

The winter of 1928 seemed interminable, and by the spring Mamie felt as though a permanent cloud was anchored over her head. Ernest was sick and often in pain. Finally, he had to have surgery for an infected gallbladder, and for nine days he lay in a coma, his life hanging by a slender thread. His recovery was slow and painful, and in those times before medical insurance, the bills ate up what was left of their dwindling cash. They had no savings, not anymore, every penny was invested in the farm. Even worse, there was growing friction between Ernest and his two older boys, something that hurt Mamie deeply. It was the oldest story in the farmers' world, hinging partly on who was boss, the boy-against-man collision of generations that was, and still is, familiar to farm families. When they left Europe for the promised land of America, Philip and Magdalena expected a place so big and free that surely nobody would need to worry about who owned what tiny parcel of earth. But some things don't change, and where father and sons share the same land, it's hardly ever big enough to hold them all.

The problem was complicated by what had become their religious obsession, so much that Mamie's third son, Len, left home and went to work for a district rancher whose daughter he'd been courting. The two younger kids felt the change acutely, sensing, as children do, an irreversible downturn, an impending sadness in their parents.

"After that," says Uncle Ken, "nothing was ever the same. And there was always some preacher and his wife hanging around, mixing in our business. They were like leaches."

And the loan shark was still hovering.

The spring of 1929 was a strange one. Even the air smelled different. The rains that usually came in May and June, the rains that were essential for the infant wheat to thrive, bypassed their land. What wheat they'd been able to scrounge for seed came up reluctantly, but without the rains it shriveled and died. Nor did the rain come in July, though it hardly mattered, for by that time the damage was done. Ernest had no crop, and even though Mamie carried every drop of water she could spare to her garden, the plants were pitiful. She could almost smell trouble in the hot, dry air.

"There'd be terrible bad thunder and lightning," said Aunt Violet, "and the clouds would roll in, big thunderheads, but no rain. Not a drop of rain. Everything died. You could pick up a tuft of grass, and it would come away, roots and all. It was the beginning of the drought, and it lasted for years. The grass didn't come back for ten years, and when it did, it was different grass.

"I remember the first dust storm. The sky turned black. Mama had to light the lamps and stop up the doors and windows or we'd just about choke to death. Even then, the dust got in. You couldn't see ten feet. My brothers were at school, and we were terrible worried. It was like a blizzard."

Mamie lived a few miles west, but she and her two youngest children, Uncle Ken and my mother, watched the same storm descend like a long night in the middle of the day.

Uncle Ken says, "I remember that dark cloud coming from the south, and in a minute everything was black. The dust sifted in through every crack. You could write your name in it."

Meanwhile, the two older boys had decided their future was no longer in farming, but in saving souls, and they left to enroll in Bible colleges. Mamie struggled on, doing the best she could, trying to ease the hard farm labor for Ernest, who was still not well.

He was barely hobbling around again when a horse kicked him, and it became impossible for him to do the farm work. The three older boys were gone. Ken, the youngest son, was not quite thirteen. My mother, Pearl, was only ten.

It was time for the fabled loan shark to make his move. In a single transaction, the entire farm was signed over to the real estate agent, for the equivalent of twenty dollars an acre—probably just enough to cover Ernest's outstanding mortgages, loans, personal notes and miscellaneous debts, including the lien. In fact, it was a fair price for that year, when the prairie had been experiencing a boom of sorts; almost overnight, the land would have been worthless and would stay that way until the Dirty Thirties ended.

In a final insult, Mamie was required to sign a co-covenant. The clerk in the Moose Jaw land titles office explained what it meant: Even though Mamie never legally owned so much as an inch of the land for herself—not a stone around her flower bed nor a shingle on the roof of her beloved house—the co-covenant also signed away her right to remain there in any capacity, just in case she was suddenly inclined to become a squatter.

And so, in the blink of an eye it was over. They lost it all. Mamie's Canadian dream had lasted less than twenty years.

Somehow, the fourth quarter of Harris-owned land belonged to Roly, so it was kept out of the loan shark's hands. In 1942 it was seized by the Crown for unpaid taxes, effectively wiping out every trace of what Mamie's family had once held as their own.

The last of Ernest's assets were his beloved horses. In desperation he'd planned to sell them for whatever he could get, an event that must have given him considerable pain, even in the planning. As it happened he was spared that chore. On the moonless night before the horses were to be loaded, rustlers ran most of them out of the corral (or so the story went), and Ernest never saw them again.

Though Mamie had more than a suspicion about who the horse rustlers were, it was a situation Ernest refused to pursue; he didn't even report the theft. My mother remembered the incident, and insisted that she too knew who had run Ernest's best horses off into the hills, but that was one story she never told in front of Mamie.

Uncle Ken shakes his head over the question of the horse rustling, says he really doesn't remember, pulls out a handkerchief and blows his nose. When he trusts himself to speak again, he tells me, "That was the end for my Pop. All he had left was six or seven of the poorest horses, and no market for them. They were probably worth less than a good dog."

All of Ernest's careful stewardship of land and animals, a lifetime of hard labor. Gone. Nothing left but dust and a few animals that were shortly to be in such poor condition that it would have been a kindness to shoot them. There are still people who shake their heads over the pitiful state of Ernest's beloved horses.

Ernest's neighbors were beginning to suffer too, not just the grain farmers, but those enterprising mixed farmers who still had a few well-fed pigs, whose hens were laying Grade A Large eggs, whose cattle and horses were quality animals, whose dairy cows were producing quantities of cream at every milking. Even these were going down the drain because they'd lost their market.

It wasn't their fault, but neither could they find a villain to pin the blame on. The cause of this part of the disaster—the failing market for agricultural products—lay elsewhere, in trade wars across national boundaries in North America and Europe.

Then on October 29, 1929, the Wall Street stock market crash was felt around the world. Wealthier, better educated, more powerful men than Ernest Harris were said to be leaping out of office windows, leaving destitute widows to grieve in their Park Avenue mansions.

When you add all of this to the prairie's growing distemper, you have an unmitigated disaster. The Dirty Thirties began rolling over the Wood Mountain district, and when they struck, they did so with vengeance.

The winter of 1929–30 was bitter, with very little snow cover, and the dry spring of 1931 turned into a summer of dust storms as the drought deepened. Farmers throughout the southern prairies told of selling two-hundred pound pigs at three dollars each, eggs at five cents a dozen, cream at twelve cents a pound. In 1931, they told of shipments of cattle returned, emaciated and half dead because nobody would buy them. By 1933, the same farmer, who had enjoyed a net cash crop of $1,614 in 1928, would make a grand total of $66.

"Wasn't long before there was so much dust it buried the wire on the fences," says Aunt Violet. "All you could see was just the top of the fence posts sticking up. . . . Seemed as though the least little breath of air would start the dust to blowing. Didn't even have to be much wind. . . . I don't know how else to describe it, but it seemed as though the earth had just got kind of fragile."

Crops failed throughout the south, and grasshoppers appeared, clouds of them, chewing through the remaining crops, making the doorstep slippery underfoot, ruining the chicken eggs. "Nobody could afford chicken feed, so chickens ate the hoppers, and then you couldn't eat the eggs. You ever smell a grasshopper? It stinks, and it's full of this stinking yellow sap, looks like tobacco juice. Well, that's how the eggs tasted."

From 1933 to 1935, winters were severe with little snow. Summers were hot and bone-dry; crop production was negligible. The year 1937 would be the worst, with record cold, no snow, no rain, severe dust storms and record summer heat.

In 1938, the prairie played another trick. That spring brought rain and a promising beginning for the first wheat crop in years. The farmers who had been hanging on by a thread rejoiced and told each other that the worst was over, but (here's the trick) no sooner had the wheat come up than hailstorms wiped most of it out. And that was just before what locals describe as "blizzards of grasshoppers" arrived to finish it off.

Small wonder if the traveling preachers in their patched revival tents pounded their Bibles and cried aloud through their tears that the seven plagues of Israel were being visited upon a sinful and unrepentant people. Small wonder if some people believed them.

But in 1929, when Ernest turned his back and walked away, having once again instructed Mamie to start packing, the worst of the drought was still to come.

Aunt Violet: "One day when Mamie was getting ready to leave the farm, Mama stopped by to see if she could help. Your grandma was standing in the kitchen with that great big kettle she used to cook food for all them preacher people, and she threw the kettle down and said she hoped she'd never have to look at it again. I think her heart was about broken."

Oddly enough, it wasn't the loss of her home, or seeing her husband sick and hurting, or even the prospect of imminent poverty that broke Mamie's heart. It was the breakup of her family. Suddenly, she was an unemployed mother, something she'd never envisioned in her lifetime.

Mamie had intended to mature into graceful old age as every good prairie woman should—loved and respected, wanted and needed, surrounded by her family. A family who would marry and live nearby, if not on the same farm then on neighboring land, and in due time would present her with grandchildren and eventually great-grandchildren. You gave your children your life, worried over them, did without for them, nurtured them all those years, but it was worth it because raising a family was like casting a stone into a pool and watching the ripples widen, one generation after another.

For herself, Mamie would have continued to plant and harvest, to cook and bake and tend her flowers and her animals, and carry on with those domestic arts that had always given her a sense of accomplishment. Now her days lacked purpose, and the empty nest loomed ahead of her like a great chasm. She felt no longer useful and very much alone.

"That was the worst part for her," says Uncle Ken. "She hated the idea of any of us kids going more than ten miles away. Nobody and nothing was good enough for her kids, ever."

Nell had been lost to her, for the college in Nampa, Idaho, might as well have been on the moon, and anyway, Nell was embarking on her first marriage. The two older boys were gone. So was Len, for although he lived only a few miles away, he had a new life, and he seldom came home anymore. Myrtle and Dot had to go out to work, and soon announced that they were both leaving the nest permanently. Myrtle would go to Winnipeg to attend officer's college in the Salvation Army, and Dot would leave to work in a Red Cross unit.

And always in the back of Mamie's mind there was that small grave somewhere in Nebraska. She no longer mourned the death of her first daughter, but neither had she forgotten, and it bothered her greatly that she could no longer remember the details of the child's tiny face.

CHAPTER 7

Anywhere But Here

*The cars of the migrant people crawled out of the
side roads onto the great cross-country highway,
and they took the migrant way west.*

–JOHN STEINBECK, *The Grapes of Wrath*

$\mathcal{F}$OR MAMIE AND THOUSANDS OF
other farm women and their men throughout the Canadian prairies,
and for others like them down across the line in Kansas and Iowa
and Oklahoma and Nebraska—for these, the dust bowl was a daily
reality. They were stuck in it, and there was no way out—not unless
they just packed up and drove away in the night with everything
portable roped to the tops of their vehicles, heading up north where
it wasn't so dry or west toward the lotus land of British Columbia.
Anywhere had to be better than here. And maybe they paused to say
good-bye to a neighbor, and maybe not because there was nothing
good about it, not one good thing, and nobody wanted to see the new
look in their eyes. The despair.

A farmer who remembers it from his own Wood Mountain
childhood tells me, "You couldn't even touch the land and it would
blow. It blew anyway. People just walked away. Some of them, like
your grandpa, never came back."

Ernest moved what was left of the family north to Assiniboia, where he somehow managed to get into the garage business. He had no formal training in mechanics, but he was a farmer, so he knew how to put engines together and make machines work and how to fix them when they broke down. It might have worked for him too, except that in all the years of his life, his timing had never been worse.

On the phone from the Saskatchewan Archives in Regina, a disembodied voice explains to me that there is no record of a garage in Assiniboia under the name of Ernest Harris. Certainly, no business license was ever issued to anybody by that name. When I explain the circumstances, she suggests that he might have become part of the underground economy that had begun to flourish on the prairies with men and women running the odd business out of their home or their suitcase, peddling their services wherever they could, bartering when there was no money to be had.

Sadly, Ernest's clientele would have been in as bad a spot as he was. Like him, they were just simple people trying to hang on, and he probably extended as much credit as he could before, for the second time in a single year, he had to walk away from a failed enterprise. Like a drowning man going down for the third time, he made one more desperate attempt to find work. Saying good-bye to Mamie and the two remaining kids, he joined the hoard of unemployed men who hopped freights.

In 1929 Canada's unemployment rate was a modest 4.2 percent. In 1930 it was 12.9 and by 1933 had climbed to 26.6 percent—more than a quarter of the population. By that winter, estimates ran as high as 32 percent.

It's 1997. I'm squinting at black-and-white pictures of men, mostly in tweed caps, often carrying bundles. A handful of faded archival photos show a ragtag army of economic refugees hopping freights, standing in soup kitchens, lining up for work in labor camps. A surprisingly skimpy record of such a critical time, but it seems few photographs were taken, either because the men weren't willing subjects or nobody cared to record that moment in history. Using a photographer's loop to magnify the fuzzy press photos, I scour the faded images, trying to pick out a face I might recognize. It's useless, of course—these men are all so young. Ernest would have been fifty-three. Not a healthy young kid fueled with energy and hope, but a sick, middle-aged man trying to jump on and off moving freight trains, competing for space with men half his age or even younger. Men who were healthy. At least they had that much going for them.

I ask my train-loving father, who had a long career with Canadian National Railways, what he remembers about what was called riding the rods. The rods in question were a number of long, steel rods attached to the undercarriage of the boxcars. They were about sixteen feet long, maybe eight inches apart and left a little more than two feet of space between them and the bottom of the boxcar.

Riding on them would have been extremely dangerous, he tells me, and with flying cinders, dirt, coal smoke, wind—well, it was no way to travel, he was certain of that. In fact, he never saw anybody actually do it, although some said they had, and he recalled that most freights had their quota of unemployed men riding illegally in or on top of the boxcars.

Apart from the considerable risk in jumping on and off the moving cars, Ernest, a law-abiding, God-fearing man, would have had to run from the railway police, the "bulls," who weren't shy about beating ticketless vagrants. I wonder how he dealt with that. How did my grandfather feel the first time he had to beg for a meal? Scared, I would guess, and humiliated, knocking on some stranger's back door to ask for bread, ask for a job splitting wood, being told to get lost. How hungry do you have to get before you can do that?

Is that why I can't seem to turn down a panhandler on the streets of my own city, now that we have them every few blocks?

After the Assiniboia move, Mamie's daughter Dot became engaged. It was her fiancé who helped them out financially as long as he could, and they spent a few relatively comfortable months in a house he owned, but before long Mamie and the two remaining children, Ken and Pearl, had moved to a second house in Assiniboia. It was cheaper than the first, and Ken remembers it as old, cold and ramshackle. To make matters worse, one of the nameless evangelists was still hanging around, demanding handouts.

Aunt Violet remembers him too. "He was a bad type, all right. I believe your grandma was afraid of that man. She finally locked the door on him."

Even if Mamie had been inclined to be charitable, she couldn't. She was flat broke. Nor had she any way of getting help. Although church groups, the Red Cross and women's organizations, such as the Imperial Order of the Daughters of the Empire, did what they could to help needy and destitute families, Mamie would not beg for charity from those she had so long supported, and as for the IODE, she considered them eastern and uppity, and had no time for them.

The disdain was probably mutual. As a naturalized Canadian citizen born in the United States, Mamie was considered a foreigner. IODE charity, which was generously doled out to those who qualified, had from its inception been designed to care for the families of British soldiers, first in the Boer War, then World War I— destitute, married women with families, who were also, in their own way, daughters of the British Empire.

There is no evidence of how Mamie and the two children survived in Ernest's absence. She told few stories about this particular part of her life, and there's no written record in the family. She did tell of one humiliating trip to the railway station, where donations of clothing and food had arrived from Ontario to be sorted and handed out by a local church. Whether she went herself or someone else had gone for her, I don't know. But she never forgot the results: "They were just a lot of dirty castoffs. Rags. A beggar wouldn't be caught dead in them. You'd think somebody could have used a little elbow grease to wash and mend those things, but they didn't. I wouldn't have them in my house."

A second boxcar revealed a bizarre cargo.

"Sugar beets, it looked like. I guess they thought we were too stupid out here, or too hungry, to notice they sent us cattle feed."

In retrospect, it's highly unlikely that the suspect root vegetables were sugar beets. Whether they were in fact turnips (for sugar beets look much like rutabagas) or just overgrown beets, the experience left a bitter memory.

Mamie's run of bad luck must have been holding because other people fared much better with the out-of-province donations. Ontario churches and farm organizations were generous with the stricken prairies, and most of what they sent was needed and useful. Two hundred and fifty relief cars eventually reached Saskatchewan, carrying second-hand clothes and sacks of everything from root vegetables to canned fruit and Jell-O powders. Uncle Ken remembers none of this, but neither has he any idea how Mamie managed for food, fuel and other essentials in Ernest's absence.

The possibilities weren't dazzling. She might have gone hungry herself so the kids could eat. She might have taken in sewing or scrubbed floors for rich women, for even during the Dirty Thirties, there were a few prairie entrepreneurs who made money. I'd like to think she became part of the underground economy, baking bread and selling it door to door, and there's no doubt that her early skills for conjuring a meal out of two potatoes and a bit of browned flour must have come in handy. But even flour cost money. Mamie had a horror of what she referred to as *going on relief.* She saw it as a degrading, shameful process, destructive to the family: "Those inspectors coming around at all hours, poking through a person's house, snooping into a person's business. . . . It wasn't right."

The stigma of going on relief was evidently more than she could bear, for my aunt insists, "Your grandma would not accept relief. She was too proud for that. She'd rather go without."

And I'm left wondering how much this fierce, foolish pride cost her. The woman at the Provincial Archives informs me that no application for relief from either Ernest or Mamie Harris was ever recorded in the town of Assiniboia. Of course, they might have applied under a provincial debtor's credit assistance clause, she muses, or maybe they just fell through the cracks. . . .

Maybe they did.

In a move that was calculated to get destitute farmers out of its hair as the Depression deepened, the federal government started a program encouraging them to head north to land that was safely out of the dust bowl. It was a homestead plan with enough financial aid to get them back on the land, but the "new" homesteads were seldom prime farmland and had often been reclaimed from others who had tried and failed.

Ernest's travels had taken him as far north as Hudson Bay Junction, a bushy, spruce-covered area of sawmills and lumber camps just south of the Pasquia Hills. His new farm was some twelve miles farther south, near a clearing in the bush called Etomami—a store with a post office and a country school, both of which have long since closed.

In the Prairie History Room at the Regina Public Library, sorting through community records of Mamie's second Canadian home, I read that Etomami is an Indian word. It means "three rivers join together," and the Fir and Etomami rivers did indeed join the Red

Deer about a mile apart, so Etomami was over blessed with water. It was also situated in a sticky black soil called gumbo, which means exactly what it says—when you add water to it, you get gum. The roads, bad as they were during dry weather, became impassable when it rained. In a final irony, Mamie and Ernest had fled the dust bowl of the southern prairies only to fall into a kind of quagmire on their northern edge.

Their new farm was somebody else's failure, covered with spruce and poplar that was only partially cleared. Part of the deal was an abandoned log house with walls you could see right through, but Ernest reasoned that it would at the very least be a roof over their heads. It was something to start with, a place to begin again.

Surrey, British Columbia. Summer 1996, with my father's sister, Aunt Bert. It's her eighty-ninth birthday, and between answering the phone and accepting floral tributes at the front door, we're drinking wine and looking at old family photos. They feature a lot of steam trains, long-closed CNR stations, pictures of my dad and mom when they were young.

Like my dad, Aunt Bert's husband was a railway man, based in Hudson Bay until his retirement. That's when they moved out here to the gentle climate of Surrey.

"When they came to Etomami," says Aunt Bert, "your grandma lived in an old log house chinked with mud. It was fairly primitive, but squeaky clean, of course. Mrs. Harris was always a good house-keeper.

"There were a lot of thunderstorms that year. And rain! It rained every day, and in that heavy gumbo soil, why of course every time you stepped out the door you were in mud up to your ears."

Mamie waded right in. I can almost hear her sighing, nattering away to the cat, admonishing Ernest to take off those muddy boots on the doorstep. Although they no longer had loans hanging around their necks, they were still dirt poor, and the world outside their clearing was locked into the Great Depression. To use one of Mamie's favorite expressions, the world was fast going to the dogs. Yet day by day, the short, stocky woman in the bib apron began cobbling together a sort of life for herself and her remaining family. Before long she had a milk cow and was making butter for Ernest to take to town and sell.

My Aunt Bert remembers: "Her butter was wonderful, everybody said so, but it was expensive—I think twenty-five cents a pound—and I couldn't always afford it."

As hard as the move was on Mamie, it was even harder on Pearl, whose early adolescence left her feeling rootless and alone. She disliked everything about the place and couldn't wait to grow up and get out of there.

Her dream was to become a nurse, like Nell, her older sister. Nell had sent her a snapshot taken in her navy blue cape with the wonderful winged hat, and Pearl had nearly worn it out carrying it around and showing it off. She'd held onto that dream since she was a little girl, ever since Nell had left home. She was determined, and she had brains and courage. What she didn't have was money for tuition or the ghost of a chance of getting it.

Uncle Ken is speaking: "Your mom was kind of drifting, I guess you'd say. There was a sort of school out there, not a very good one, and Pearl was taking a higher grade than they offered. Correspondence course. She was smart, you know, but the teacher didn't want the extra work. She and Pearl had a fight, so Pearl quit school. It was a darn shame. She was only fourteen."

My mother at fourteen. A dropout. No job. No marketable skills. No future.

One day, two years later, Uncle Ken stopped at the store in

Etomami and fell into conversation with a young man who was managing it in the owner's absence. Gene Godin was a handsome young French Canadian with dark, curly hair and the quietly reserved manner of someone who was almost painfully shy among strangers. He was a telegrapher for the CNR when there was work for him, but he'd been laid off again, so in the interim here he was in Etomami, managing Tom Gilmour's Red and White store.

Uncle Ken had been planning to take his younger sister to a dance that night, for Pearl was sixteen and bored. He asked Gene if he'd care to come along. The evening must have been a success because the following summer, on July 27, 1936, he and Pearl were married. She was seventeen years old.

Meanwhile, Mamie's new home was little more than a mudhole, and no matter how hard they worked, there seemed to be no measurable progress. One spring, fed up with the whole thing, Uncle Ken knew he had to get out, get away, if only for a while. He headed west to the Okanagan Valley, where out of sheer luck he located a piece of land. Not just any land, not another mudhole or dust bowl, but good, productive land. Overnight, Ken's future went from bleak to hopeful. It was the most exciting thing that had ever happened to him in his entire twenty-eight years, and he could hardly wait to share it with Mamie and Ernest.

"Pretty as a picture, that valley. Flowers, fruit trees, why I'd never seen anything so beautiful. It was like a dream. I wrote to the folks right away and told them about it—wanted them to come and join me. But Mom wouldn't do it. She said she'd made her last move, and of course Pop wouldn't come without Mom. I think the real reason was because she couldn't stand to leave Pearl. Even though Pearl had got married, they were still real close. She was very attached to Pearl."

So he went back, reluctantly, to the mudhole in Etomami.

Mamie stuck it out on the Etomami farm, but she never liked it. It was as though the good years in Wood Mountain had been a dream. Sometimes her whole past life took on an air of unreality: how could they have lost it all, everything they'd worked so hard for?

As the years passed, Mamie made do. Things began to get a little better—they acquired a radio, and in the evenings she listened to *Fibber McGee and Molly,* and sometimes in the afternoon, ironing or baking or doing some of the endless mending, she'd turn on the trials and tribulations of *Ma Perkins.* They could afford a newspaper again, so the *Free Press Prairie Farmer* and the *Family Herald* came back, for she loved to read. She made a few friends, and as she grew older their names popped up in her stories and in her handwritten recipes—Mrs. Drechsler, Mrs. Knutson, Mrs. Jervis, Mrs. Halliday, Mrs. Binkley.

Although they were at least marginally better off than when they'd left the dust bowl, Ernest seemed somehow dispirited. Mamie noticed that he looked different too. He was a big man, six feet and well filled out, but now his clothes hung on him as though they were too big, and his skin took on an odd pallor.

That fall, on a day when he was probably too sick to be out of bed, he tried to do some farm work and was seriously hurt in an accident. Accidents are so much a part of farm life on the prairies that it's never a surprise to meet men with fingers or hands missing. A farm has always been a hazardous place, rife with opportunities to be poisoned or maimed or suffocated or crushed. In Ernest's case, it was a log that rolled on him, crushing his leg.

For as long as she could, Mamie denied her worst fears, as humans do, hoping the nagging doubts that disturbed her sleep and came ever closer during her waking hours would go away. Ernest wasn't eating well, and when she finally screwed up the courage to ask the question, he had to admit what she already knew—that his stomach hurt almost all the time, and the pain seemed to be getting worse and lasting longer.

Mamie, realist that she was, would have said a desperate prayer. *Not Ernest. Dear God, not Ernest . . .*

Ernest and Mamie, circa late 1946.

CHAPTER 8

The Long Good-Bye: Easter 1947

"Guess now who holds me?"
Death, I said, but then the answer came,
"Not death, but love."
—LAST ENTRY IN MAMIE'S CASH BOOK
(*Paraphrased from* Sonnets from the Portuguese)

HE WINDOWS IN MAMIE'S TOWN kitchen were high up in the wall, too high for me to see out, but I could feel the breeze when it ruffled the curtains. It was a tiny house that had been owned by my father when he and Pearl were married, and when Ernest could no longer stay on the farm, he and Mamie moved into it.

The kitchen was only big enough for a table, a woodburning cookstove and a washstand. There was no plumbing, but a little green pump stood at the sink, and it only needed two or three vigorous up and downs of the handle for water to come gushing out in great, cold gulps. There was a cellar under the kitchen, with a metal ring attached to a trap door in the floor, and I fell in once, all the way down the stairs—*You scared everybody half to death, especially your mother, she thought you were a dead duck*—although I don't remember the incident at all.

As I grew up, my cellar caper would be recalled by Mamie and my mother at the stove or by the ironing board. It was trotted out as ammunition for a cautionary tale whenever I wanted to do something vaguely dangerous, like ride my bike on the highway. *Remember the time she went head over heels down those stairs? My land, we all thought she'd broken her neck.*

Although I spent a lot of time in Mamie's kitchen one winter, I don't remember much serious cooking, and none of the big family feasts like the ones on my father's side of the family. But then it was not a time for celebratory meals, for my grandfather was slowly dying.

Now it's Good Friday. Mamie and I are alone because my mother is still at the hospital. (She must be or she'd be here with us; I think she's been gone all night.) Mamie stands by the stove, wearing her good black dress with an apron over it, and she's stewing something in a pan of milk. Her eyes look at me without really seeing, and when I tug at her apron to get her attention and demand to know what she's cooking, she says just one word: "Oysters."

When she finishes cooking, there isn't much in the pan, and it fits nicely into a small sealer. She wraps the jar in a dishtowel, ties a three-cornered knot for a handle and puts on her good tweed coat with the velvet collar. At seventy Mamie is about to say good-bye to the man who has been with her through everything, for better and for worse, since she was eighteen. She takes my hand and we walk out the gate and turn left, past Beattie the Nurse's house, past Aunt Bert's place, past the last house on the street where the sidewalk runs out, and into the jack pines, where the big stucco building stands. (In the Prairie History Room of the Regina Public Library, I find a photograph of the Hudson Bay Red Cross Hospital, and although its gabled roof and slope-shouldered shape is exactly as I remember it, the building looks small, much smaller than I remember.)

Judy (nine months), Pearl (Harris) Godin, Eugene Godin.

Through the front door, through the scary smells of ether and disinfectant, past the woman at the desk, stiff white hat, stiff smile—*Hello Mrs. Harris*—down the hall, brown linoleum, very shiny, and into the quiet white room where my grandfather waits.

There's only one bed in the room, and it's high off the floor, so I stand on a stool to talk to him, but for once he doesn't seem interested in me. His big hands pluck at the sheet as though something too heavy is leaning on his chest, and he makes odd, whimpering noises, like a hurt animal. Nurse Roebuck sails in carrying a hypodermic needle on a little tray. While she gives my grandfather a shot of morphine, I stare at the laces in her white oxfords, terrified that I'm next.

I have a brown paper bag with gumdrops in it, and there's a black one, which I've saved for him because they're his favorite. We always play a game over who gets the black one, except not this morning. Mamie says, "Not today, honey. Your Grandpop doesn't feel so good."

The whimpering stops, and Mamie unwraps her jar of oyster stew, and the meal begins. One by one, slowly and with infinite tenderness, she feeds him the soft gray oysters in their pale sauce, wiping his lips with her handkerchief between bites.

I CAN'T REMEMBER there being any words between the two of them, and nobody talked to me, except about the gumdrops. It was years before I understood that this strange, silent feast was for Mamie a sort of ceremony, a final gesture of love.

I've since wondered, why oysters? They'd never lived near an ocean, never even visited one that I knew of. Maybe the oysters were from another time, another country, when they'd been young and hopeful, looking at life from the other end. Had he, during some long ago hour of pillow talk, promised her the whole world, and had she replied that someday she'd like to see the ocean? Maybe then he said, *Yes, sweet Mamie, you will have the ocean, two oceans if you want, and we'll have a feast, and eat oysters just like the rich folks.* And so on and so forth, the way lovers do, whispering away into the night. Or had some grasping-at-straws doctor told her to try to build up his strength with soft, nutritious things? Oysters would be good. Lots of zinc. And so, somehow on that Easter weekend in 1947, in a small town in rural of Saskatchewan, she found them.

January 1996. Hunched over a table in the Prairie History Room,

I spot a name on a page that triggers a memory. Dr. Silver. Dark, wavy hair, a thin, black mustache, black eyes. That morning in 1947, his soft hand patting my cheek—not hard and callused, like my grandfather's, but soft like my mother's. He scares me even more than Nurse Roebuck, and I know by Mamie's face, when he arrives quite suddenly at her kitchen door, that he's scaring her too.

It's EASTER SATURDAY and Aunt Bert appears, whisking me off to her house to sleep over. This is fine with me because Aunt Bert lets me play with her jewelry and try all her perfume at once, and she calls me Lovie. (She still does, though I am comfortably middle-aged and she is nearly ninety.)

On Easter Sunday she's up early, rattling around the kitchen, making pancakes especially for me. Neither my mother nor Mamie are anywhere to be seen, and in spite of chocolate eggs and some thin-sounding stuff about a rabbit in a red suit, I can feel a silence in my own small world filling the space where once there was a familiar voice. I know with the clear-eyed certainty of a child that Mamie's one and only love has died in the night.

I WONDER NOW how much of the man who was my grandfather is my own memory and how much is family myth, the man they talked about, Mamie and Pearl, until he became bigger than life itself. I don't remember how Mamie mourned the loss of her husband. I was too young to be included in those rituals, whatever they may have been, but in my memory her stocky little figure began appearing and reappearing in our household with greater frequency and for longer visits. It seemed that she no longer felt at home anywhere, and had entered a kind of limbo.

Sometimes it would be Pearl and me, going to visit Mamie in Hudson Bay, jolting along for hours in the lone passenger car that

CNR attached to their freight trains. I can still feel the night air on my face as my mother hustled me down the steps, and I was passed to Aunt Bert and suddenly enveloped in a cloud of Evening-in-Paris. Aunt Bert was more than my father's sister—she was also my mother's friend. She wore bright red lipstick even at that hour, so I knew that our late-night arrival was worth getting dolled up for, and I loved her for it.

Soon there would be the warmth and light of Mamie's tiny house, and the smell of cocoa and toast, which Mamie made by impaling a slice of homemade bread on a long-handled fork and holding it over coals in the cookstove until it smelled good and changed color enough to suit her. Sometimes the butter had brown sugar and a wisp of cinnamon whipped in, and it became the most wickedly delicious thing I had ever eaten so long past my bedtime.

Those visits had a distinctly feminine texture that I enjoyed enormously. It was a world peopled only by women—Mamie and my mother, Beattie the Nurse from next door, my Aunt Bert popping in for tea and chitchat. Soon Mamie began spending winters with us, and once I went home with her for the summer to her tiny house in Hudson Bay. She promptly enrolled me in Vacation Bible School, where I excelled at macaroni art—glued a picture of a lilac on a slab of plywood and alphabet-macaronied the shortest Bible verse I could find: "Jesus wept."

She praised it extravagantly and hung it up, and then we baked a cake and carried it to her friends, old Mrs. Jervis and her rather slow-witted daughter, Irene. I remember a feeling of great privilege and luxury as the four of us sat in the sun porch among the leggy begonias, debauching gently over Red Rose tea and vanilla sponge cake with wild strawberries that Irene and I had picked in the woods behind their house.

By this time my father was a station agent with Canadian

National Railways, and like many railway families, we moved around a lot. Dad, my mother, Pearl, me, and whatever cat or dog was currently in residence and my little brother, Bud, who didn't arrive until after I'd turned seven, so I was an only child for a long time. And eventually, Mamie.

With all our worldly goods rattling around in a boxcar, we traipsed from province to province, Manitoba to Saskatchewan and back again, shuttling across the prairies so often that I learned to dread the idea of another move, of once more being the new kid on the block in another tiny town where nothing ever happened.

The names of those towns still rattle around in my mind—Arran, Margaret, Kamsack, Mafeking, Hallborough, Englefeld, Quill Lake—though except for the last one they no longer have any particular order. Kamsack, an early Doukhobor settlement just inside the Saskatchewan border, was the metropolis of the lot, having nearly two thousand citizens at the time. Hallborough, in Manitoba, was so small that its population was halved when our station house burned down and we departed, leaving only four others—two McKees and two Novacks—to hang on until they too packed up and left, and Hallborough disappeared from the map. At last count, Margaret, in southern Manitoba, had a dwindling population of some twenty people.

For the rest, they were much alike, each with a block or two known as Main Street, running from the wide-open space of a farmer's field at one end to the natural boundary of our station house and the railway tracks at the other. In most of them, there were a couple of streets on either side of Main, and somewhere between the farmer's field and the tracks would be a school, a church, a general store, a post office, a lumberyard and a hotel with a beer parlor and cafe, frequently run by the only Chinese family in town. Just across the tracks from our station, standing tall and aloof in a row of their own, would be the prairie versions of skyscrapers: the grain elevators. Two or three in most places, five or more in the heart of the grain belt. These, along with the church, school and general store marked our progress and validated our existence as a community worthy of being named on a Wheat Pool map and supported by the surrounding farms.

I suppose I remember the towns best by crisis. Kamsack: a kid named Jerry lured me onto the roof of our building, where I was found and summarily spanked by my terrified mother. Arran: I was the only child in town who didn't speak Ukrainian. Englefeld: the only Protestant in a Catholic school. Hallborough: our house burned to the ground and my cat ran away. Mafeking: physical brawls in the school yard, me and Sweetpea Baron against the ferocious grade two Mafia, led by the teacher's only and badly spoiled daughter, Jo-Anne. Margaret: my brother was born, I found friends and I cried buckets because we had to move again.

In the childhood society of small prairie villages I was the perennial outsider, plunked down among them well after playground friendships and classroom alliances had already been forged. My role seemed predestined. I was to be teased, baited, stared at, giggled about and generally tormented until I'd feel so sorry for myself that I'd start to sniffle and then to howl, and would go tearing home, all red-eyed and runny-nosed, to make my poor mother miserable.

Pearl couldn't cope with my whimpering. She felt every hurt I felt, but with a difference—I compensated, as children do. Once I reached the refuge of our railway house—where I knew I was safe, cherished and had access to a bottomless cookie jar—I was content to play alone, designing clothes for a mammoth collection of paper dolls and planning playground revenge with imaginary friends, the ones who moved with me from town to town and could be counted on for sympathetic conversation whenever I needed them.

No sooner would we vacate one town for another than I'd be struck by a bout of nostalgia, longing for the familiar rhythms of the enemies and territories I already knew, rather than having to brave yet another pack of hostile strangers.

I doubt that Pearl shared her concerns for me with my father, but in later years I learned that she had worried about me because I talked to myself. Listening to the strange conversations her daughter was holding with nonexistent companions, I think she feared incipient and permanent oddness in the rather solitary child I had become. From time to time, during brief lulls in my ongoing social crises, she would decide that I was at last beginning to cope and maybe everything would be all right after all. But then I'd fall through the back door rumpled and tear-streaked with a fresh tale of humiliation or intimidation at the hands of some new school yard villain, or my father would announce that we were moving one more time, and she'd start worrying all over again.

It was Mamie, watching this procedure during one of her frequent visits, who took me aside and delivered her simple message in a firm and compelling tone. I've never forgotten what she told me.

"Stop sniveling, honey. You'll survive."

She said it with complete confidence, like a doctor issuing a prescription, which if taken as directed would cure whatever ailed me. It was a code that had worked for her, and probably she'd passed it on to her own daughters before me. Without any doubt, it was the best advice a nomadic prairie child could have received, and it has been useful on many occasions since.

The sink-or-swim mentality of those small, ill-equipped and often ill-administered schools taught me a whole gamut of survival skills for the society in which we lived. By the time we landed in our final village, the one we stuck with until I went away to university, I knew enough not to dissolve into tears every time I suffered some real or imagined injustice, and I could hold my own in the political hotbed of the school yard. If in the end I became more the passive observer than active participant, I was also the survivor that Mamie advised, and mine was, I think, a good childhood, enriched with the company of pets and books and a family who loved me.

And yet, never belonging anywhere, I suppose I must have been lonelier than other children. In leaving childhood behind, I closed some doors I no longer care to open, and I wonder how much those early gypsying years and their attendant solitude shaped my inner landscape, and if it's what drives me now, searching for my roots, somewhere on the prairies.

What happened, I wonder, to the Novacks and the McKees, and to the red Chinese poppies in my mother's garden, now that Hallborough is no longer on the map? I wonder too about Margaret, the village with the one-room schoolhouse, where I learned to read and write and an entire universe was suddenly opened to me. What happened to the tiny formal park with its cenotaph for two world wars and its magnificent caragana hedge, so splendidly overgrown that local kids had worn a path right down the middle, offering us the great luxury of privacy from curious adult eyes? And the tiny post office run by Suzie Lancaster's granddad, who always smelled of pipe smoke? And Cotter's General Store, where Johnny Cotter's dad sold everything from rubber boots to all-day suckers and chocolate ice cream?

They disappear, those tangible chunks of prairie history, but where do the intangibles go? Surely all that energy, that life force of hope and prayer and dogged tenaciousness that informed their beginnings must be fluttering still, hovering somewhere over these prairie places long after the highway signs have been taken down and the names have disappeared from the map.

I'm not sure how to deal with the months and then the years

when Mamie was part of our household. Were we richer for that enforced togetherness, that mingling of three generations under one roof? Certainly I was and probably so was my little brother, Bud, whom Mamie adored. But he was much younger than I, and being a boy, he was never occupied with those domestic tasks that drew women together, the skills that both Mamie and my mother felt were essential for my orderly progression from childhood to womanhood.

Mamie had reached that unenviable stage of a woman's life when, deprived of the male figure who had always defined her role as wife, mother and companion, she was no longer valid. Widowed and growing old with no means of support beyond a flimsy pension, she needed a place to live where somebody cared about her. It was Pearl who undertook the responsibility, and for her those years were harder than I could have known or understood at the time. My father put up with the intrusion of his mother-in-law into the privacy of his home and his life, but not without some natural reluctance. There's no doubt that Pearl was torn between the opposing needs of her husband and her mother, and her loyalty to Mamie was hard on their marriage. As I grew up she often made a point of telling me that she would never live with one of her children—*Never ever, not even if I have to sleep under a street lamp.*

Mamie and my father tolerated each other in a politely civilized way, and to their credit I never heard one of them say a mean word about the other. An uncomfortably silent truce ensued, and year in, year out, the full extent of their conversation amounted to *Good morning, Gene* and *Good morning, Gram.*

Throughout those years, it was Mamie, coming and going on her visits and eventually taking up residence upstairs in our guest room, who gave me a sense of place. Without knowing that she was doing it, she taught me to see the beauty in wide-open spaces, to feel their freedom and to love the infinite variety of the prairie's distinct seasons. In retrospect, I know it was through Mamie's prairie-born credo—stop sniveling, you'll survive—that my own truth slowly dawned: I wasn't an outsider—I was prairie, just as much as the gophers or the elevators or the snooty kids in all those little towns. Whatever and wherever the greater scheme of things might be, this was my place. It was where I belonged. That sense of belonging to the prairie somehow became implanted in me as surely as my own genetic code, so I knew that I was forever a part of it and it of me. Not of a town, not of a school or a choir or a team, but of the prairie.

CHAPTER 9

At Eighty:
1957

*T*HE CHRISTMAS WHEN MAMIE WAS
nearly eighty, I watched the night train drop the usual sacks of mail
and potatoes on the platform of our railway station house and roar
away into the east, toward the bright lights of Clair and Wadena.
Shortly afterward, Mamie and I were summoned to the freight shed.

A dim, chilly room with deep shelves along both sides, the shed
had its own smell, a heady blend of all the things it collected over
the years: onions and cabbages, rubber tires, apples, baby chicks. On
that particular evening my father handed me a big cardboard box
with two names on it: Mamie E. Harris and Judith L. Godin, Quill
Lake, Saskatchewan. In the upper left-hand corner were the words
Harry and David's Royal Riviera Pears and a curiously lifelike sketch of
two men. They looked thirtyish and healthy in their plaid shirts, and
I could see by their smiles that Harry and David enjoyed the services
of a good dentist. Until quite recently, I still received a Harry and
David catalogue each Christmas, and they still grinned at me from
the inside cover, the picture of expert dentistry and eternal youth.

Mamie and I didn't waste time with formalities—we ripped open the box and found it lined with a cloud of soft, silvery stuff. Nestled inside were two dozen pears, each one individually wrapped in purple foil. Harry and David had enclosed a nice card inviting Mamie and me to join their Fruit of the Month Club and informing us that the pears were from Nell, my exotic aunt, far away in California with her third husband, her cat and her own grapefruit tree.

The only husband I'd met was the third and present, who accompanied Nell on a visit the previous summer. My little brother, Bud, and I had ample opportunity to study him at close range, as he didn't seem to mind kids hanging around his Chrysler. He had a passion for oversized cars and loud plaid shirts, which he felt were *de rigeur* when traveling as far north as Canada, and he had a disconcerting habit of grabbing the nearest female relative and bear hugging her to his broad plaid chest, bellowing, "Gimme a hug, sweet thang! Gimme a little shugah!"

My father and Mamie watched these displays with narrowed eyes. During all the years Mamie lived under Dad's roof, it was probably the only time they were ever in total agreement on anything.

The new uncle seemed to be an expert on almost every subject, especially food, and when he said he had a present for me and dived into the trunk of his car, I expected a chocolate bar or maybe a grapefruit from Nell's tree. Imagine my surprise when he came up with a tiny jar of funny-looking things that turned out to be pickled artichoke hearts. I thanked him, and Bud and I listened while he expounded on artichoke growing in the Salad Bowl of Civilization, which was his pet name for the Salinas Valley, where he and Nell lived.

I tried to trade my artichokes for Bud's water pistol, but he wasn't interested. Then I tried to give them to Mamie, but she said it was a sin to give away a gift, so I knew she didn't want them either. Every now and then I'd give the jar a little shake and watch my artichokes roll around, but as gifts went they ranked right up there with a new toothbrush.

One day Bud and I were in the backyard helping him admire his car when he made one of his periodic dives into the trunk and came up with a bag of buckwheat flour. Right away we smelled trouble.

"I'm gonna make y'all a batcha the world's best hot cakes," he yelled, shattering the quiet of the Saskatchewan morning. My dog started to bark, and Mamie appeared at the kitchen window, wearing a face like a fried onion. I considered telling him that my father already made the world's best hot cakes once a month or so, except, being Canadian, we called them pancakes, and that Dad might not be thrilled to learn that his only competition was The Windbag (his term) Nell had married on the third go-round, but it didn't seem like anything the new uncle would want to hear, so I kept my mouth shut.

The hot cakes took a long time. There was a lot of commotion in the kitchen, with spilled milk and buckwheat dust everywhere. Mamie noted this grimly, to Pearl, in a loud whisper, "Land sakes, just look at the mess. Why the kitchen will look like a chicken coop by the time he's done." There was a lot of giggling while Nell tied one of Mamie's aprons around his considerable girth and got bear hugged nearly to death for her trouble.

When the new contenders for the world's best pan/hot cakes were finally loaded aboard our Sunday platter, they were stunningly ordinary in a dry sort of way. My mother declared them "interesting," and Mamie chewed thoughtfully and said, "My, my!" And once she said, "Mercy!" but it wasn't clear why.

My father smiled grimly, and thereafter referred to the visiting uncle as "That Windbag Your Aunt Married *this time.*"

Nell, whose only fault was her habit of marrying the wrong

men, watched the whole performance and said nothing, but I could tell she was thinking hard. So when the Royal Pears arrived at Christmas, Mamie and I decided that was the reason. Because of the pancakes and probably the bear hugs.

After Christmas, Mamie seemed to bloom. She bought herself a new gray coat and a matching hat with a red feather and a plane ticket to California. Maybe she wanted to check up on Nell's delicious lifestyle, or maybe she just wanted one honest to goodness adventure of her own. In any case, we all piled into Dad's Ford to drive her to Regina, where she'd catch a flight to Los Angeles, and as we waved good-bye and the plane taxied down the runway, I could see the red feather bobbing gently in the window.

Mamie sent me a postcard with an orange tree on it. In her pointy script she'd written, "Having high old time in California. Wish you were here." When she got back she announced that she was moving out. She had found her own apartment.

For a year or so, she lived in two rooms tacked on the side of Haggard's big old house near my school. For her those two small and rather drafty rooms represented a kind of freedom she'd never had, removed from the sadness of the Hudson Bay house and the old ghosts of the past. She lined her windowsills with plants and began growing African violets, a hobby that became a passion as she acquired pots of Pink Fluffy Ruffles and Evening Star. When we bought her a pair of noisy budgie birds for her birthday, she named them Dickie and Belle, and hoped they would mate. Belle, a gentle bird with gorgeous blue plumage, could do nothing to please Dickie, who was green, spiteful and coldhearted. When Belle turned up her toes and died, possibly of a broken heart, Dickie ruffled his feathers and kissed his own image in the little mirror we'd hung in his cage. Mamie forgave his vanity, but she never got him another mate. Not long ago, rifling the pages of Mamie's old Bible, three slender, green-tipped feathers fell out. Holding them, I could almost hear Dickie screeching in his unmusical voice, and Mamie chirping back, "Pretty bird, pretty boy."

On my way home from school I'd fly through her door to bombard her with the big events of my life over tea and cookies, and sometimes I'd find people there, two or three old ladies visiting over the teacups, laughing like schoolgirls. It seemed to me that my grandmother had found her niche.

On Saturday mornings, bribed by the promising aroma of chicken soup, I'd give her floor a cursory mopping and a coat of Johnson's Glo-Coat, and then we'd make a batch of fat, pillowy noodles and eat a smashing lunch with red Jell-O for dessert. And all the time we would talk, for if there was anything my grandmother liked better than a good pot of chicken soup, it was a lively conversation. The world was surely going to the dogs, and the least we could do was discuss it.

I've said that Mamie gave me a sense of place, but it went beyond that to include a sense of my own history. During her old age, in the years when she was so often my companion of an evening, she'd look at my textbooks and snort. Like most Canadian children of that era, I'd grown up steeped in the history and geography of other peoples and other places while remaining ignorant of my own.

Much of what appeared in our textbooks was irrelevant to the cultural backwater of small prairie towns. In my grade three reader, little girls in frilly dresses strapped wheels to their feet and skated on smooth cement sidewalks while in the real world we bundled up in snowsuits and skated on ice. I wondered: If you stick your tongue on the bottom of a roller skate on the way home, does it get stuck?

In grade five I'd memorized the names of every American state, along with its major cities and principle industries. I could parrot off *Ohio: Dayton, cash registers; Akron, tires,* in a dreadful little monotone as though chanting a catechism, and Mamie said it stood her hair on end.

Although she was proud of her American heritage, and never lost her faintly midwestern accent, her real loyalty was to the country that had taken her in and been her home for so long. She became a Canadian patriot though never a monarchist. She thought the royal family was a waste of time and tax money for Canadians and said so, just by way of information, while helping me paste clippings from the Saskatoon *Star Phoenix* into a scrapbook of Princess Elizabeth's marriage to the Duke of Edinburgh. She mused that it was a strange thing indeed to have a Canadian grandchild who could tell her more than she'd ever want to know about the Boston Tea Party, but who did not understand the Riel Rebellion or the Medicine Line and didn't know diddley-spit about a man named Sitting Bull.

Mamie found ignorance offensive, so during winter evenings in her room, and on Saturdays over the chicken soup during her freedom summer, she had gradually educated me in my own long overdue history. She told me many things. About wick lamps that were made with a twisted rag dipped in oil and didn't give enough light to read by, but kept the boogiemen from scaring her on a dark night. About dolls made of corn husks and toy boats made of walnut shells and vinegar pie that was almost as good as lemon, when lemons were scarce as fur on a sparrow. About making butter and keeping it down the well so it stayed sweet. About coloring Easter eggs with water from boiled onionskins, beets, dandelion leaves . . .

She told me about winter storms when men got lost in their own backyards and never found the house. About two little girls who got lost because they didn't listen to their mother, and only their bones ever showed up near a stream that has ever since been called Lost Child Creek.

It was Mamie who told me about the buffalo. I already knew

about them from the history books and considered the mythical beasts irrelevant, but the way she told it, they were vital, massive, woolly, snorting herd animals that should be part of the natural heritage of every prairie child. She explained how they'd been here for the longest time, before the cattlemen came, before the Indians came to the plains, before the first pyramid was built in Egypt. How their shovel-shaped heads could dig for grass beneath the deepest snow. How if they felt threatened they formed a tight circle, facing the enemy like the good parents they were, with calves protected in the middle. How just a few years before she arrived in this country, thousands upon thousands of them had stampeded through the very coulees where her homestead was soon to be. How a herd could be so big that it would take a whole day to pass a single point, or so she'd been told by Big Joe, who had seen it happen. And how they'd disappeared suddenly, these prairie giants, wiped out by a bunch of greedy men, and when they were gone, so was a whole way of life that had been good for a lot of people and could never ever come back again.

She knew these things because she'd lived among their abandoned drive lanes and on their killing grounds, for she'd sometimes found their bones and even their great white skulls during her early rambles over the prairie. And there was the rubbing stone, a big boulder up on the ridge, where they used to scratch themselves because being a buffalo was an itchy business during the heat of summer. "Flies were terrible bad. Mosquitoes too, and then they'd get awful hot under all that wool, and they'd get fleas and ticks." I've seen and photographed a lichen-covered rubbing stone in the west block of Grasslands Park, but Mamie's rubbing stone has disappeared from our family map along with a certain teepee ring she knew about, and Shelf Rock, a broad sandstone outcrop where my brother and I once found Pearl's name scratched in the soft stone when she was a child. We were kids ourselves at the time, so we added our own names but we've not been able to find Shelf Rock since.

Mamie had discovered a buffalo wallow, a depression in the earth about ten feet across and four feet deep. The wallow was some distance behind her house at Wood Mountain, in the lower part of a hillside, and she explained how the whole herd must have chosen that particular spot to roll in the dust and cool off. The wallow had been another kind of back scratcher, softer by far than the rubbing stone, and it was still there when she arrived, even though the last buffalo had been gone for twenty-five years. For a brief time each spring, the wallow became a puddle. Mamie said it wasn't big enough to be a slough, or even a pond, but the puddle stayed just long enough for the new crop of goslings to adopt it as their private swimming hole.

She had her own piece of prairie history too. A special rock, a grooved and rounded sandstone she'd found on one of her rambles. She used it as a doorstop, and Mom called it her Indian hammer. I decided it was a war club because of the groove that ran all the way around it where a thong had apparently fastened it to some sort of handle, and I got a morbid thrill out of holding the rock in my hand and imagining how many skulls it had split.

She corrected me on that one too. *It's a maul,* she told me. *A meat hammer. The Indian women used it to pound meat after the buffalo hunt. It was the woman's job to cut up the meat and load it on the hide, and then she'd drag it back to her camp, and she'd get her maul and start in to make the pemmican. Didn't I know about pemmican? Didn't they teach me anything in that school? War club! The very idea. . . .*

One of Mamie's stories was about Old Wives Lake, the large inland sea she'd first seen on her trip south from Moose Jaw to Wood Mountain. *That lake was so salty it would float eggs. Neither man nor beast could drink the water, but there were always birds resting there, gulls and pelicans and what not, coming and going. Some people saw ghosts out there on the lake. At night they'd see the fires. . . .* She made it clear that they weren't really ghosts at all, but a handful of old Cree women who one dark night had cleverly lit a lot of fires and scared a band of Blackfoot warriors into thinking they were outnumbered, or so the story went. Sometimes people saw things on the lake or thought they did—bands of men walking or on horseback. Sometimes when the wind blew just right, people said they could hear the old wives crying or laughing.

In the summer of 1988, for no apparent reason, Old Wives Lake suddenly dried up, leaving scientists and politicians scratching their heads and pondering the odd mirage. The few farms around the lake and the single industry of the sodium sulfate plant that once opened on its shores were abandoned. Now, in wet years when there's water in the lake, it has a tendency to develop an algae that kills waterfowl. And if the ghosts of a few old women still light fires at night, there's nobody left to see them.

CHAPTER 10

Good-Bye Again:
1961

$\mathcal{T}$HE SNOW CAME EARLY ONE YEAR, on Halloween. Within a week, a full-fledged winter came howling into town, and suddenly the prairie changed from the warm gold of autumn to the stark black and white of a northern winter. The wind cried around the eaves and piled snow against the door of Mamie's lean-to apartment, drifting across her sidewalk, making it impossible for her to get around with any sort of ease. My dad dug her out regularly, and kept her woodbox full, and we got her mail and shopped for her groceries. I still dropped in after school, but somehow it didn't matter. Within weeks she seemed to shrink, which was hard for a woman who had barely cleared five feet on her tallest day. Her energy was ebbing, and in late November she moved back into the room above the railway tracks.

The late Truman Capote, when he described life as being like a play with a bad third act, might have been describing Mamie's life at that point. For her part, she simply felt that the world was once again going to the dogs, and this time it was taking her with it. For a while she tried hard to be a presence in the kitchen, helping with the Christmas cake, the mammoth dark fruitcake that had been Mamie's recipe from an English neighbor in Wood Mountain. Fruitcake was essential to our prairie Christmas along with steamed carrot pudding, Scottish shortbread and mincemeat tarts, but she didn't have her usual enthusiasm for these culinary rituals.

It wasn't any one particular thing with Mamie. She just began to wear out. The day came when she could no longer see to whack up the bird for her chicken soup. Her arthritis was bad, and climbing up and down stairs had become a chore, so she began spending less time in the kitchen and more time upstairs in her room that looked out on a Pool elevator. Her heart was, as she said, "giving her fits," and the times when she'd suddenly have to sit down and pop a nitroglycerin pill under her tongue grew more frequent. Finally, she gave up coming downstairs every day and began having most of her meals on a tray. In spite of her retirement from active kitchen duty, she always wore an apron with a bib and two pockets, as though expecting to be called back to the stove at any moment. Mamie's apron was part uniform, part armor and, as the most frequent tray bearer, I noticed that she never ate a morsel unless she was wearing it.

During that winter, Mamie and Pearl tried hard to teach me the skills every prairie woman needed to have. I was encouraged to sew until I'd made half a dozen identical aprons, all with identically crooked seams. My knitting was a flop, and the scarf I confidently started became narrower and narrower, the stitches tighter and tighter, until Mamie gave up and decided I might as well try crocheting. It was the Year of the Afghan, and they were working on a big one, black-trimmed squares with rainbow-colored centers. As the blocks mounted up, mine were consistently rejected—I dropped stitches, mismatched colors, lost the hook. What I liked to do was read, and in the end that's what I did, night after night as they stitched away.

Among Mamie's most remarkable qualities, the one that stood out was this: She minded her own business. "Thank the Lord that I can think and not be heard," she would mutter when she was itching to comment on some domestic issue that arose within our household, but she would not interfere, and she did not pry. Over the years, that was one reason I spent so much time in her room.

The winter of the Christmas pears, Tim, my big orange tomcat, had died an untimely November death. In January I found him frozen stiff behind the garage, awaiting spring and a decent burial. All that winter, in the blue-snow afternoons between school and supper, I would stand among the frozen cabbages, whimpering over my dead cat until my nose began to drip. Had my mother noticed the tears, there'd have been an official inquiry, explanations would have been demanded, and it would have been noted (correctly, I'm sure) that I was far too old to be crying over a dead cat who, after all, had been in pet heaven for months.

But upstairs in Mamie's room, grief was a private matter. Life could be cruel, and nobody knew it better than she.

In spite of her semi-exile, Mamie was a sociable person, and on Saturday afternoons she had company for tea. Usually, it was just old Mrs. Sayer, who had legs like stovepipes and huffed and puffed all the way upstairs, so I'd go up with her and hang around, listening for hot gossip until my mother called me to come downstairs and get the tray. It was always draped with what she called fancywork from her endless store of embroidered flour-sack tray cloths. On Saturdays she got out her Royal Albert china and the silver sugar tongs, and served lump sugar instead of the plain, granulated kind we used the rest of the week. Her baking powder scones were legendary, and she'd pile them on a plate while they were still hot with the butter melting into little yellow puddles, and a saucer of chokecherry jelly on the side. Mamie could no longer eat the jelly because her diabetes was out of control, and she'd fold her lips into a thin, tight line while she watched fat Mrs. Sayer wolfing down the scones, but she never protested aloud.

Still, I knew she hated missing out on all the sweets. One Sunday night when she thought we were all at church, I found her downstairs in the kitchen attacking a jar of strawberry jam with a big spoon. Caught red-handed, she was furious and not about to apologize.

"Getting old is no fun," she snapped, slamming the lid on so hard I figured we'd never get it off again. "Help me upstairs and don't you dare tell your mother."

Even now I can hear the despair in Mamie's voice, her bewilderment at her failing body, at the injustice of the inevitable.

"You get old!" she raged. "You get old. This is what it comes to. . . ."

Her diabetes grew steadily worse, and inoperable cataracts had left her nearly blind. Her tricky heart was acting up too often, and the doctor informed my mother that Mamie's arteries had narrowed dangerously. Her bones had brittled too, as female bones will do in old age, so he hoped she wouldn't fall. In the mornings when I took hot water upstairs for her bath, her room had a stale, musty, *old* smell, and I didn't like it any better than I liked her false teeth grinning at me from a glass.

There was another aspect of Mamie's rapidly declining health that bothered me, and it had to do with my own future, as decided by my mother Pearl, my Aunt Nell and Mamie: after high school, I would go to a school of nursing. Thus would past dragons be slain: my mother, who never had the chance to fulfill her own dream, would get her wish vicariously, through me; Nell, who had no children, would see her mentor role fulfilled as I followed in her foot-

steps; and Mamie would at last stop grieving over Pearl's lost education, for which she felt personally and sadly responsible. All three of
them agreed that an education was the best insurance a woman could
have, and they intended to see that I enrolled in a good school of
nursing.

The older and sicker Mamie got, the more often I heard both of
them talk about my upcoming and no doubt illustrious career as a
latter-day Nightingale, for according to them, I belonged to a mysterious category of female known as the Born Nurse. *That girl is a born
nurse*, they'd say, usually after I had accomplished some astonishing
medical feat—handed Mamie a pill or rubbed her hands when her
arthritis bothered her or pasted a Band-Aid on my little brother.
Nell seemed to concur, and I still have her envelope with an American date-of-issue commemorative nurse stamp and a long letter in
her pointy scrawl about the joys and rewards of my chosen profession. Nobody, not even in passing, ever suggested that as long as I
was going to take the nursing profession by storm I might just like
to take a crack at medical school and become a doctor. It was the sixties and the rural prairies, and I was just a girl.

The only fly in the butter was my own profound disinterest in
their project. Oh, I was keen enough about wearing a cute white hat
with backswept wings enhancing my profile. And I could definitely
see myself swishing through the streets of some cushy foreign resort
in my navy blue nurse's cape, saving lives and marrying doctors in the
best tradition of the nurse heroines in the Harlequin Romances my
mother had lately taken to reading. I was less pleased to deal with
the nitty-gritty of the job, as evidenced by the simple nursing care
that Mamie now required and I refused to give.

What I hated most was the daily injection. This was my mother's job, but by the time I was fifteen or sixteen she decided it would
be a good thing for my impending career if I'd prepare and admin-

ister the insulin shots on weekends just for practice. Mamie didn't
object although on many occasions she probably wished she had.

For my part I hated boiling the glass syringe and the metal needle
in that little aluminum pot, putting them together with the sterilized
clamp, arranging the tray with the alcohol, the gauze, the chilly vial of
insulin we kept in the fridge. Even though insulin is an intramuscular
injection, I was terrified that I'd get an air bubble in the syringe, hit a
vein and kill her. I was almost equally terrified of hurting her, so that
instead of a quick, clean jab, I'd make two or three tentative pokes at
her arm or her thigh, loathing the meaty resistance of skin and flesh
before finally gritting my teeth and forcing the needle in (but slowly,
slowly). Mamie always declared my injections to be totally painless,
and thanked me afterward, and then she and Pearl would congratulate
each other. *She gives a good needle,* they'd say. *She's a born nurse.*

In the fall, Mamie decided to make one more move. She needed
more care than my mother could give her, so together they visited a
senior's lodge in the next town, came home quiet and subdued, and
packed Mamie's belongings. My dad wrestled her favorite chair and
her reading lamp into the trunk of the Ford and off she went. "I'll
spend the winter in the home," she said. Then, she'd see.

The Family Album

*Mamie and a friend at Christmas, in her room at Waneeda Lodge for Senior
Citizens, better known in our family as The Home. She's wearing a new navy dress
with confetti-colored polka dots and the rhinestone broach I gave her for her birthday. Behind her is a pitcher filled with some of the fir boughs my dad hacked off the
bottom of our Christmas tree. Mamie sits on a wooden chair from the common room
because a guest—old Mrs. Somebody whose name I can't remember—is parked in
Mamie's own chair. Her reading lamp is behind the chair, and on the wall, tucked
into the corner of a framed print, is a picture of me. Mamie is smiling, and I
remember The Home as a cozy room in a friendly place staffed by local women who*

probably did their best to keep their charges well fed and comfortable. I think she seemed happy there.

Mrs. Somebody and Mamie in her room at The Home.

When the prairie spring was beginning to show itself at the end of April, we brought Mamie back and checked her into the little hospital in our village. The snow had melted early that year, and there were purple crocuses poking through the winter-brown grass south of the railway tracks. Usually, she'd have been thrilled to hear about such an event, but not this year. She'd lost interest in the changing of the seasons.

In the hospital Mom and I took turns sitting with her in the single ward at the end of the hallway reserved for the dying. She was still conscious when her bed was wheeled in, "Just so you can have a bit more privacy, Mrs. Harris," the nurse said, fooling nobody, least of all Mamie. Probably we made small talk, a little nervously, the way people do while waiting by the departure lounge to see a friend off on a journey. I just remember holding her hand.

We were all waiting for one more visitor—Len, the son she hadn't seen for thirty-one years, the only one she'd left down there on the prairie. Her prairie. He came, as lost children do when they realize the clock is ticking on a parent and something needs to be said, some last few words, difficult as they may be after so long a time. He stayed an hour and then got in his car and headed south again, back to the solace of the prairie, unable to wait with the rest of us. But it was enough. When he left, it was clear that Mamie had taken care of whatever unfinished business they had, and she was at peace with herself.

In the late afternoon she lost consciousness as though she'd had enough of our chattering about things that really didn't matter to her anymore because she was about to be off on her next journey. Sometime before midnight on April 20, just a few months short of her eighty-fifth birthday, Mamie Elizabeth Harris drew one final breath and died.

After her funeral we all piled into the large car from Narfason's Funeral Parlor and followed the hearse northward for hours, all the way to Etomami, so Mamie could be buried beside Ernest. I didn't like taking her there, leaving her up north in a part of the country where nothing good had happened, where she'd never felt at home. One of the religious uncles blurted that "Pop's been waitin' here for her since 1947," and I wanted to hit somebody.

At the Etomami corner, a procession of cars was lined up, waiting. Farmers and their wives, people my parents' age, dressed in their Sunday clothes. They'd probably waited a long time on the still-rutted road that led to the second farm, the one she'd never liked, and I was thoroughly glad to see them. The men all took their hats off as we drove slowly past the corner, and every car turned on its lights as they swung in behind us. *Hey, Mamie, they remember you!*

The graveside service was short, and then a crowd went back to Aunt Bert's, where a lot of people told me I was the spitting image of my mother at my age, and I remembered that at my age my mother was already a married woman. Aunt Bert put on such a spread that it would have been a first-rate wake, except that it was a dry party out of respect for Mamie.

An ordinary woman who'd lived so quietly for so long and asked so little had gone out in style, with her own parade and a smashing tea party. It was a toothsome bit of irony, and I know Mamie would have enjoyed it.

THE FALL AFTER MAMIE DIED I dutifully entered the College of Nursing at the University of Saskatchewan. At that moment Pearl felt that her dream, the one she and Mamie had shared, was coming true at last. My unfortunate mother could not have predicted that the closest I would come to being on the wards during my first year was a twenty-minute hospital tour and a rather pointless class called Nursing 101, an abbreviated history of the pathetic state of European womanhood during the Middle Ages. The rest of the time I was just a freshmen doing the only things that really mattered to me: dating, going to parties and hanging out at the library with my friends.

Still, it wasn't until my second-year anatomy class that Pearl's vicarious nursing career went up in smoke. By the time I'd spent a winter lugging pickled cadaver parts around a crack-of-dawn anatomy lab and loathing every second of it, I knew I was in the wrong profession. I began wasting hours in the medical library, looking for some obscure, painless disease that wouldn't be disfiguring, debilitating or life-threatening, but would get me out of my hospital hell.

Epilepsy? Amnesia? I was saved the further ignominy of faking a rare and unpronounceable form of glandular fever by the simple expedient of failing the anatomy class and being given only a conditional pass in physiology. I topped it off by putting a patient's watch down the laundry chute, misplacing somebody's false teeth and tagging a man for major eye surgery when he'd been hoping for a simple appendectomy. All of this on the same day.

The dean of nursing, Hazel B. Keeler, delivered a stern ultimatum that involved pulling up my socks and getting my nose to the grindstone, but no matter how many bracing clichés she employed, I'd heard them all before and we both knew this was a waste of time. By some miracle they didn't kick me out that day, possibly because of the dean's other favorite cliché, one Mamie had used a lot: *Where there's life, there's hope.*

In desperation I appealed to my father, who found himself stuck in the middle between the two women he loved most. He must have hated having to mediate, but eventually he came down on my side. I have no idea what passed between him and Pearl over the issue, but it was with a great sigh of relief that I turned in my uniform and walked out of my nightmare in nurse land. Lacking the guts to tell her in person, I called my mother to give her the news, and I can still hear the painful silence that fell between us that day.

Why is it that out of love and the best of intentions we so often make our children's lives utterly miserable? A mother's dreams for her children are always bigger and more important than her own, holding as they do all of the love and hope that begins the moment she hears their first cries. I shattered Pearl's dream and broke her heart, but she never blamed me and never mentioned it again.

My inglorious departure from the nursing profession wouldn't have been so hard for her if we'd still had Mamie. The two of them would have talked it all out by the ironing board or the sewing machine, with Mamie's rocker going *squeak squeak,* and in the end they'd have had tea and decided to stand by me in my disgrace.

Mamie in her gently compelling way would have convinced her that I might still amount to something, if they just gave me time.

But Mamie was gone, and my mother's unswerving loyalty to me kept her from discussing my shortcomings with her friends, so she grieved alone.

CHAPTER 11

The Circle Complete:
Pearl, 1990

*P*EARL WAS NOT JUST MAMIE'S DAUGH-
ter. She'd been in many ways and for many years her closest friend.
Partly because of how often my parents moved and partly because it
was her nature to be rather solitary, Pearl made *me* her closest friend
after Mamie died.

For years we were each other's cheerleaders. When she became
chairman of the local school board, I was proud. When, at fifty-
something, she went out and got herself the first job she'd ever had
and began collecting a monthly cheque, we were both over the moon.
The day my first son was born, she looked at his little jaundiced
prune-wrinkled face and cried because he was so beautiful. And she
told me how when I'd been born twenty-four years earlier—prema-
ture, jaundiced, weighing four pounds and not expected to survive—
my father had held her hand and declared me beautiful. When I sold
my first story to a magazine, she was the first person I called. As my
writing career developed there were times when she didn't like what I
wrote, and she told me so, but she always defended my right to say it.

Often in those years we talked of Mamie, and the years the three of us had spent together, and sometimes it was almost as though she'd never left.

Like Mamie, my mother was a realist, and in the fall of 1990, although she was only seventy-two, she knew she wouldn't live much longer. She began giving things away, things that mattered to her and should, she felt, be passed on to somebody who would appreciate them. Bud's wife, Joyce, got her china. I got her silverware. When I protested that she still had years to live, she told me to stop being ridiculous and face facts. I could hear Mamie's voice: *Stop sniveling; you'll survive.* That's when Pearl gave me the grandma ring, the wedding rings that had belonged to Magdalena and Sophia, then to Mamie and eventually to Nell.

After Mamie's death, distance and circumstance often separated Pearl from her remaining siblings, but as her illness grew worse she often turned to her sister Myrtle, Mamie's third daughter, for comfort. Myrtle was another of my favorite aunts because, although she held the same rank as her husband in the Salvation Army, she never lost her slightly wicked sense of humor.

Writing had become difficult for Myrtle and impossible for Pearl, who could no longer hold a pen, so the telephone became their medium. I wasn't privy to these conversations because they liked to talk in the evening, after the daily trials of visitors and hospital routine were over and they were free to be just the Harris girls again. I imagine they spoke of husbands and children, of loud neighbors and indifferent food, and how getting old was no fun. They'd have wound up by agreeing that nobody listened to them anymore, and declaring that without their guidance the world was well and truly going to the dogs. During the late hours of Pearl's life, when there was nothing left for her to do but mark the inexorable passage of time, those long-distance visits with her sister redeemed what would have otherwise been the longest, loneliest nights of all.

One day as I sat beside her bed, she told me exactly how she wanted it to be: "No heroic measures. I don't want them bringing me back as a vegetable. Don't let them do that to me." And no funeral. Pearl hated the trappings of death, the public tears and the mourning and the undertaker creeping around all solemn and whispery, "As though he really gave a hoot about anything but lining his own pockets. . . . No undertaker is wintering in Hawaii over *my* dead body."

No grave either. No burial. I remembered then how she'd hated Mamie's graveside service, and she said so afterward. She didn't like enclosed spaces at the best of times, and the very idea of her earthly remains being lowered into a grave and covered up with dirt had always appalled her.

"I want to be cremated. You see that your dad does that. Or you arrange it. Don't you let anybody stick me in the ground."

Cremation appealed to her on many levels, not the least of which was this: she'd at last be free of the body she no longer trusted or even liked very much because multiple sclerosis had left her virtually helpless.

During her long illness she'd parted company with organized religion, and she told me firmly that the rest of this life and whatever else was to come later on was strictly between her and the Almighty. So no minister either.

The night she died, I'd been with her until around two in the morning. I was napping in a small waiting room around three o'clock, when a young resident came in and woke me up. "I think you should come now. She's in failure."

In failure? What exactly does that mean? The implication burned into my sleep-fuddled brain. *What do you mean, she's in failure?*

The woman is DYING, for God's sake. This is not a test. She is not, and never has been, in FAILURE. What a pathetic term, how woefully inadequate. A last-ditch excuse by a profession devoted to prolonging life at any cost, one that had never learned to deal gracefully or even humane-ly with the natural transition we call death.

But there was still a little time, so we waited together in her cur-tained cubicle. About five o'clock a ward aid wandered through the curtains with a sheaf of paper menus, wanting Pearl to decide on tomorrow's dinner. "Meatloaf or fish," she twittered determinedly. "Red Jell-O or pineapple surprise?" We gave her a mutual glower, so she scurried out, curtains and menus flapping, and we grinned a lit-tle crazily over the irony of tiny minds turned loose in huge hospi-tals. *Excuse me, I know you'll be, ah, gone by dinner, but if you'd just fill out this menu anyway. . . .*

During the last hours of her life Pearl and I talked because it was our lifelong habit to do so, and probably because we found a certain comfort in the sound of each other's voice. When speech became too tiring for her, I talked.

I remember rattling on about dogs because we'd had so many between the two of us. Tuffy and Pogo and big George and the Spot-ties, which sounds like a B-circuit rock band now that I write it, but was in fact the big black mongrel and a series of fox terriers that had shared both our lives and Mamie's. *Remember how that crazy fox terrier used to steal Mrs. Foster's chickens? Remember Pogo's sassy face? Remember?*

I think husbands were mentioned, mine and hers. And children, mine and hers. Neither of us mentioned Mamie, but I suppose she was in the back of Pearl's still-conscious mind as she was in mine. Mamie had never really left our exclusive club of three though she'd definitely been quieter during the past years. In that hospital cubicle, with its state-of-the-art machines hissing and blipping, and the green light that monitored Pearl's heartbeat making its irregular way across the screen, I don't think I'd have been surprised if Mamie had suddenly materialized at the other side of the bed. *No sniveling*, she'd say. After all, we were only tying off another thread in the cloth she'd begun weaving so long ago.

It was still dark outside when the green light on the monitor gave a sudden, fickle jump and then flattened into a long, straight line, and after that Mamie's daughter had no further need for her reluctant heart.

The Rest of It

CHAPTER I

Waiting for Something to Happen

How will we know it's us, without our past?
—Ma Joad, John Steinbeck, *The Grapes of Wrath*

Summer 1996. Walking southwest of Wood Mountain in the heat of a July noon, reading the land. Those sandstone layers, that cap rock, the yellow lichen, the angle of the outcrop just ahead—they're like words in the story of how this prairie was built, layer by layer. In my hand is an gnarly length of diamond willow, silver with age, an old fence post from Mamie's garden. My brother, Bud, found it earlier this week as we prowled around the old homestead, and I thump the ground with it as I walk to warn off rattlesnakes, hoping that most of them are coiled up in the cool of some unhappy gopher's underground burrow, hiding from the heat of the day.

Mamie knew this place as the Killdeer badlands, and some of the local people still call it that, though it's marked on the map as the East Block, Grasslands Park.

"You're going into them badlands? You watch for rattlers in there." So says Aunt Violet in Rockglen, and she's not kidding. At the marker to the park, detailed instructions regarding rattlesnakes are posted. Leave them alone and they'll leave you alone, the notice assures me. Rattlers are shy and human intruders are unlikely to cross paths with one. In the event that I do, and should I rile one by accident and find myself on the receiving end of a bite, I'm advised to stay calm, the notice says, and get to a hospital as soon as possible. Do not use a tourniquet; do not cut or apply suction. So much for my brother's old Boy Scout manual. Bearing all of this in mind, I thump along with my diamond willow, eyes to the ground. Farther in, written notices are replaced by yellow markers with a life-size picture of a coiled rattlesnake.

Though I walk for hours, I see neither hide nor hair of anything resembling a rattler, and it's doubtful that many people do. Another official pamphlet lists them as provincially rare, along with the prairie long-tailed weasel and the elusive sage grouse. In fact this piece of southern prairie Mamie loved so much, with its sparse vegetation and beautiful, contorted landscape, has become the last refuge of a number of once-plentiful species of reptiles, mammals and birds.

Plovers, thrashers and the gentle burrowing owl, common enough in Mamie's day to have figured in many of her stories, are on the endangered species list, facing imminent extinction unless their luck changes fast. The Baird's sparrow and the loggerhead shrike are considered to be "threatened." So are all the sassy black-tailed prairie dogs, plump little rodents tumbling about the burrows of their prairie dog town, hugging, boxing, chattering at each other from one house to another in their neighborly way as you'd expect of the citizens of any prairie town.

The graceful, long-billed curlews are also threatened and the Cooper's hawks and the fierce-looking ferruginous hawks with their wonderful plumage and the falcon and the golden eagle, the great gray and the short-eared owl. Mamie knew them all—they were part of her prairie, inseparable from it, or so it must have seemed, but time and circumstance have changed their very existence.

Except for here, in the grasslands, where they coexist amiably enough, largely due to the absence of humans. In the first two weeks of July, the year's busiest tourist month, only thirteen people have signed the park's guest book. The officially designated East Block of the Grasslands Park is, like the West Block in the Frenchman River Valley, a chunk of native prairie that was first set aside in the eighties and is gradually being enlarged as land is accumulated from district ranchers on a willing-seller basis. There's no road into the East Block, no facilities or drinkable water in either block. Such water as there is flows in the small, insecure creeks—Hellfire, Horse, Rock, Weatherall, and a few other creeks. They rush along the bottoms in wet years and are apt to disappear completely when the rains fail.

Few plants can tolerate such a climate for long, yet as many as one hundred varieties of grass manage to survive and even thrive in this hostile environment. Prickly-pear cactus is coming into bloom now, its tightly closed buds still red and swollen, its opened blossoms translucent, as pale and delicate as butter-colored silk. I step lightly over clumps of bunchgrass and tufted spear grass growing from powdery brown soil, but with each step my boot heel leaves a clear impression, reminding me once again just how fragile is this rugged-looking landscape.

My path crosses the prairie, flat as a tabletop, and ends abruptly at the edge of a deep coulee, its broad floor a moonscape peppered with gray hummocks, odd-looking shapes whose smoothly rounded tops were carved long ago by rivers of ice, by the water that once went coursing through here and by the omnipresent wind. At their base, swirls and eddies of pure white mark the alkali salts in the soil. This valley is a dinosaur graveyard, the first recorded remains having been found in 1874 by one George Mercier Dawson, a British geologist serving on the original version of Her Majesty's British North American Boundary Commission three years before Mamie was born.

This has been a wet summer, and the surrounding hills that in a normal year would already have taken on their customary toasted look are still green, but down there in the coulee the colors are all muted, a palette of earth tones: silvery-beige, every shade of brown—cinnamon, chocolate, rust, brindle. As the day wears on, the colors change dramatically, softening as the changing light washes over the valley.

The wind has been blowing steadily these last two days, hissing along the edge of the cliff, singing up from the valley, whistling around the outcrops in that strange musical way that is peculiar to this part of the country.

Now, as evening falls on the third day, the wind drops and in the sudden quiet every sound comes sharp and clear. Off to my right, the chattering of a gopher who feels I've invaded his space. A metallic clicking—some sort of beetle. There's bird music, trills and tremolos ringing sweetly in the stillness, one song so different from the other and with an uncanny order to this impromptu symphony, as though the meadowlark waits for the killdeer's solo to end before jumping in with her own.

A pause now in the bird song and I turn in a slow circle, a full 360°, watching, waiting for something to happen, to twitch or jump or flit, as things will do here when you least expect them. Nothing moves. Not so much as a blade of bunchgrass bends, no cactus flower quivers under tread of bug, no bird or animal crosses my sight line. A strange sense of timelessness and my own insignificance in the scheme of things settles over me, and it's as though these outcrops, this landscape that Mamie loved, has been here forever, immutable, constant, frozen.

Yet six hundred million years ago, this place on which I stand likely straddled the equator. I say *this place,* but I mean this whole great sprawling prairie, as far as I can see in every direction, to the faraway edge of the grasslands and beyond. At first it would have been barren rock, but time and again the waters of warm, shallow seas washed over it and receded, and covered it again and receded again, first the Dunvegan Sea, followed by the Wapiti Sea, the Milk River Sea, the Lower Belly River Sea, the Upper Belly River Sea and finally the Bearspaw Sea, so on and so forth into the centuries. Each time the water level fell, it left its sediment behind with the corpses of rudimentary sea animals piling one upon the other, pressure becoming compression, until layers of limestone and dolomite formed.

And then the prairie-to-be shifted south, where strange, multi-legged creatures with exoskeletons crept out of the sea. The first plants appeared, and as they breathed their photosynthesis began to raise the oxygen level. It had taken two hundred million years, but at last, the miracle: Life was happening.

By the Devonian Period, the prairie-to-be was again on the move, this time sliding even farther south, hot and dry as a desert, and in its shallow tidal flats evaporation was swift, so the sea salts concentrated into broad, pale lagoons of potassium chloride, to be known as potash. This salt was a legacy, for a time would come when the mixed-grass area of the dryland prairies would contain more than half of all the potash in the world.

Those primitive vertebrates that would evolve into multiple species left the sea for the land, but it took another sixty-five million years for the land mass to begin its long journey back toward the equator, where even then a massive subcontinent was forming with amphibians and giant reptiles roaming the land.

Two hundred million years ago, the great subcontinent began to crack, and as the fissures became fractures and giant chunks broke off, the prairie-to-be was swept north, and again the seas covered it, leaving deposits of marine plants and animals that would with time decompose into petroleum.

By the Cretaceous Period, the mighty dinosaurs were in their last days, and the sediments of the last seas formed the vast bedrock that would soon underpin the prairies. But there was more to be done, for now the land was greening. Warm, humid, it was covered with lush, subtropical jungles of ferns and palms, bog-growing plants and cedars, and when the great trees died and fell over they didn't decay completely, but instead formed the porous mass we call peat. More time, and the deadfalls continued to pile one upon the other until the peat was compressed into lignite coal. As the Cretaceous Period ended, the soon-to-be-prairie gave a last mighty heave, shifting one final time and fetching up in the general latitude it exists in today.

By the Tertiary Period, a mere sixty-five million years ago, the continent had risen from the surrounding seas and the folding and wrinkling of the earth's crust we call the Rocky Mountains had begun. After ten million years of giant reptiles, their sudden disappearance had left a void in the ecology, and mammals began to thrive on the land that was at last a prairie.

Even then its face would continue to change. The ice age would scour it with successive glacial and interglacial periods, eroding, shifting, leaving debris behind, with the meltwaters of the receding glaciers running south, carving great fissures into the bedrock, broad, deep river courses that would become the Frenchman and the Milk River. Today, only the height and breadth of their deep valleys gives the casual visitor some idea of the mighty waterways they once were. The scrubbed face of the prairie offered few obstacles to the almost constant wind, which would continue to erode its surface for another ten thousand years before the first human came along to notice it.

With sea levels dropping and the land bridge forming between Asia and North America, herds of early mammals were free to wander: mastodon and mammoth, bison and bear, giant cats, deer, the doglike wolf. Behind them, following the food source, came another traveler—humans—arriving at last on the prairies just twelve thousand years ago. Not so very long as these things are counted. Like the dream chasers who would come from somewhere else to settle the prairies at the turn of the century, the first people here were immigrants.

Walking the prairie now, I'm clutching that diamond willow stick that was cut by one of my own immigrant ancestors nearly a century ago while it was barely more that a sapling, and it feels good in my hand. Warm and solid. Dependable. In youth, this gnarly old stick became a fence post on a piece of land my ancestors dreamed into gardens and fields, carefully, deliberately marking each plot of newly-turned earth according to some hopeful vision in their own heads. Wheat here, potatoes there, a spot for flowers later, when there is time. Like all dream chasers, they thought they could shape this land, so for them a fence post seemed more useful than a tree, and for a time maybe it was. Yet in the end it was the land that would shape them, the land and the climate, and as always on the prairies, the final arbiter of everything would be the wind.

CHAPTER 2

A Sense of Place

I may not know who I am,
but I know where I am from.
—WALLACE STEGNER, *Wolf Willow*

*T*HE NAME OF A PLACE SHOULD BE
self-descriptive if its to be of any real use, and prairie places have
always had names like that. They are what they say they are, and a
Willow Bunch or a Rockglen, a Swiftcurrent or a Whitemud Creek,
should have no other name than that which so eloquently reflects its
particular state of being and maybe its history. The best prairie
names are like that.

Wild Horse Creek says it all. So does Wood Mountain, Maple
Creek, Grasslands Park, the Killdeer badlands, Skunk Butte or Lonesome Butte for that matter, or the places known simply as the Buffalo
Jump, of which there are several. They appear on smaller tourist maps
under that name for reasons familiar to prairie people, and nobody as
far as I know has ever tried to call them anything else, except for Head-
Smashed-In, which lies across the Alberta border. Even that name tells
its story of the Indian boy who thought he'd stand under the cliff and
watch as the giant beasts tumbled to their deaths, and how he was
found, suffocated by the falling animals, with his head smashed in.

Prairie places take their best names from the animals and birds and plants, things that were naturally and rightfully here long before government surveyors, politicians and royal visitors began traipsing around the district, acting like bureaucrats. For instance, a saskatoon is a fruit that grows on the grassland prairies and up into the parklands, so that the only people who have eaten it and learned to love its winy sweetness and slightly bitter seeds are prairie dwellers. It's a good, descriptive name for a Saskatchewan city. Pile of Bones also was a good, descriptive name for a town that once had a small white mountain of buffalo bones lining its railway track. It was a name that had panache and a certain memorable ring to it. Who could ever forget visiting a town with such a name? But it lacked something, elegance maybe, so nothing would do but to change the name, and it became Regina, which commemorates the ten-minute visit of a royal personage, but what does it evoke of the history of the place? And what does it say about the rich heritage of native, Métis and white who gave the place its reason for being? For the reality of the prairie, past, present and future, is its capacity to play the magnificent leveler. Airs and graces will not impress it, whimpering will not move it. It tolerates survivors; no others need apply.

Like Mamie and Pearl, I'm comfortable with the minimalist landscape of the prairies, with its harsh, sudden seasons, with the things that are born here and survive here. Like both of them, I cherish the long, luminous evenings of summer, a season all the sweeter because it's so brief, and I plant things for the sheer joy of watching them grow. In the fall some primeval force urges me to squirrel away supplies for the coming winter, so I haunt the farmers' market where women not unlike Mamie still sell their garden produce, their baking, their patchwork quilts and woolly mitts and dried bouquets. With difficulty I restrain myself from buying cases of tomatoes and sacks of cabbage.

The winter is the prairie's own love–hate relationship with its people. Like everybody else, I hate the inconvenience of stalled cars and reluctant traffic. But I love the tranquillity of the winter landscape, the muffled silence of the early morning, the sight and sound of falling snow, the long blue shadows of the late afternoon. Like a prairie animal snug in its burrow, I'm somehow thrilled at the howling, shrieking force of a good two-day blizzard that brings out survival skills and those good-neighbor instincts that get so little use among contemporary urbanites.

Around the beginning of April, when the days have lengthened and a softer, warmer wind carries the green smell of poplar sap, I still sense, deep within my bones, the excitement of a newly hatched season. It's as though every joint in my body has been freshly oiled, and a great rush of hopefulness goes coursing through my veins in the certain knowledge that once again anything is possible.

Is it reasonable to become emotionally attached to a landscape, even to a climate? I've read that when a bird is hatched, it will claim the first thing it sees as its mother, be it duck, dog or rabbit. So I think it must be with places, for the prairie claimed me early, as it did Mamie and then Pearl. Having identified with the prairie in childhood, I am to this day so thoroughly prairie that I feel like a tourist anywhere else in the world.

I live now on the prairie's edge, just a comfortable drive from the Rocky Mountains, but when I'm in them I'm overwhelmed, overawed, and I start buying postcards. When I'm by the ocean I feel giddy with pleasure, thrilled as travelers are when they've landed somewhere faintly exotic and subtly alien. Either way, mountains or seaside, I'm just a traveler passing through, a voyeur peeking in the lighted window of somebody else's room. It's only on the prairie, where so many travelers see and feel nothing but the great emptiness, that I feel well and truly at home.

Its such an old landscape, this one, yet its contours change and are renewed with every passing cloud. The prairie can be cruel, and it has broken as many as it has embraced, probably more, yet there's something about its undulating hills and huge, painted sky that excites me. It makes me feel strong and hopeful, and gives me a sense of freedom I never experience anywhere else in the world.

CHAPTER 3

Where the Chips Fell

Let the chips fall where they may.
—OLD CLICHÉ

*N*OW THIS BECOMES A BOOK THAT IS as much about *where* as it is about *who*. The prairie defined its people, especially its women. It gave them a special look, windblown, sun-tanned, and they wrinkled early, their faces weathering as their skin acquired the color of walnut. The prairie also decreed how the women would relate to the land and to each other, and it initiated them into the sisterhood of next-year country, of boom and bust, so they always knew that no matter how good things might be at a given moment, some other small thing might come along and bring a big, unwanted surprise. Grasshoppers maybe, chewing so fast and so hard through a field that you could hear the sound of their tiny, dreadful jaws at work and within hours your crop would be flat on the ground with nothing left but a few sprigs of straw. Or rust, the fungus that left the wheat looking strangely robust from far away, that gave it a sort of rosy glow until you got close enough to see the red blisters on the stem and knew there'd be nothing left to thresh. Or August frost, hard and killing, turning a bumper crop into feed grade overnight.

This is what I remember. At the time it impressed me more for the resigned sadness I felt in one of my uncles than for the reason behind it.

It was our August holiday some time in the fifties. My Uncle Len had the best crop he'd ever had. "You could almost see it grow," said this man of few words, who seldom expressed optimism about anything so iffy. The field could be seen from the kitchen window, rolling and shimmering in the wind. He'd take off the best crop ever, and my quiet uncle, who never said boo about anything, told us this with real pleasure over the fried chicken and coleslaw at supper.

Sometime after midnight the prairie pulled one of its sneaky tricks, the little temper tantrums that add up and up, piling one small, freakish disaster upon another until they break a man. The temperature started to fall fast. When it hit −12°, it bottomed out for an hour or so, and then gradually started working its way back up, so by ten o'clock the sun was shining and the day was as warm and soft as you could ask of any late summer morning. But for the wheat, it was too late. It was finished. He stood by the window, looking at his frozen crop, not saying a word, and the pain of his silence filled the kitchen, settling over us like that frost.

His wife spoke a few words born of a prairie woman's experience: "Well now, at least it's over. If it wasn't frost, it'd be rust or some other dang thing. . . . Now at least it's done with."

Even before the frost, there was always the possibility of drought. On the prairies, drought is the worst thing, especially in the 850,000 square miles that made up Palliser's Triangle because without water nothing would thrive. The dust bowl had taught them that. And all of this put together became the basis of their prairie creed, which was based on that old cliché about never counting your chickens before they were safely out of the eggs.

The prairies even gave the women a way of speaking that is peculiar to the area: a soft, lilting drawl that Mamie never lost, neither southern nor exactly midwestern, but somehow naturally prairie. It also gave them a vocabulary that is theirs alone, so when they talk of a coulee, a rise, a butte, a ridge or a hogsback, they will be understood by others who know this land and misunderstood by those who don't.

SUMMER 1996. Wood Mountain. Betty Thomson is a blue-eyed prairie poet with curly, graying hair, an easy laugh and a sense of place that runs so deep she doesn't even recognize it herself, except when she's writing her poetry.

One July day I phone Betty to introduce myself and get permission to take some horses across Thomson land. She quickly identifies me as the writer who's been wandering around the district, researching a book, something about local history. (My aunt has been on the phone.) Betty offers to act as a guide on our trail ride, pointing out that we'll never find the place we're looking for unless somebody local goes along. I figure she wants to make sure that a couple of greenhorns don't wreck her fences or leave her gates open, a legitimate concern among ranchers dealing with city folk. A visit seems in order, and I invite myself onto the Thomson place so she can check me out in person. She's almost visibly relieved when she meets my husband, a tall, quiet man who knows his way around a farm and tends to inspire confidence.

Four or five dogs and a couple of horses range around her front door, and she yells at the cavorting dogs to get down (they don't), orders the curious horses to get outta here (they don't) and points out the newly installed fence protecting her flourishing petunia bed from the livestock. This morning she sprained her ankle in a gopher hole, and she winces painfully when she steps on it the wrong way. In her living room she shows me her photo album and talks of prairie things that touch her deeply.

"It's funny, but there are two extremes here: people who can't get out fast enough and people who'd never leave. I have always felt attached to the land. This was my folks' chosen land, their Eden, their paradise. We thought it was the most beautiful place on Earth."

Mamie used almost those exact words when she'd talk about the old homestead. Recently, as I walked among the azaleas with Uncle Ken in his lovely coastal garden, I asked him to describe the homestead as he remembered it, and he said the same thing: "We thought it was the most beautiful place on Earth."

Not the most beautiful place in western Canada or even in North America, but on Earth. Without doubting the beauty of the Eiffel Tower or the pyramids, prairie dwellers also know with complete certainty that for them this is the best, the most beautiful place this side of heaven.

"There's lots I'd change," says Betty Thomson. "The horses are always hanging around the yard, and they eat my garden, and sometimes when the wind blows so long and it seems like it'll never rain again, I do wonder . . . but there's nowhere else we'd rather be."

There is a small but articulate lobby of activists—mostly naturalists and ecologists—who feel that people like Betty Thomson and her family shouldn't be here at all, and that Mamie and *her* family should never have put a plow in this prairie earth. They point to worrisome statistics on the degradation of the native prairie with its fragile and rapidly altered ecology, and they argue convincingly that these grasslands should never have been ranched, let alone farmed. The zero-tolerance group within their ranks would turn it back to its original inhabitants, the buffalo. I ask how she feels about the movement to reclaim a lot of this land.

"I love the natural prairie. The grass. I've seen it up to the bottom of the saddles, and the men on horseback looked like they were floating, floating in grass. . . . Every plant out there, I could tell you its name. I could show you wild animals. Badgers. Deer. I've stood at the spring and watched a deer come for a quarter mile, and it didn't scare when it saw me. I've watched Harold pet an owl. It was sitting on the gate, watching the dogs, and Harold motioned me to stay still, and he walked right up to it, real slow and quiet, and touched it. It flew about ten feet to another post and then settled again."

She pauses, reflecting on that particular small miracle, and then continues: "Our land is sand. The topsoil is shallow. It's hard at times to get it to catch back into grass. But I like to eat, and I believe we have a moral responsibility to feed other people in the world. So we need to have a balance in how we deal with the land, and sometimes that's pretty hard to find."

THE NEXT DAY, another perfect, midsummer morning, on the little bay horse named Slicker, I ride the hills somewhere south of Wood Mountain. My brother, Bud, rides ahead, half turned in his saddle in case the horse or I get in trouble. Slicker, my niece's horse, is a champion barrel racer and he's not fussy about greenhorns, but it's a pretty day for a walk, and the clover smells toothsome.

Betty's ankle is worse than yesterday, so her husband, Harold, rides with us. Three or four Thomson dogs and my brother's blue heeler range around us, running back and forth, grinning as only dogs can in a sort of canine ecstasy with only their waving tails and an occasional pair of ears visible above the grass. With Betty following in her truck so she can handle the fences, we head over the hills toward the site of the old Bayard School, the one some of Mamie's kids attended, including our mother. This is mostly Harold's land now, and he knows it as well as Mamie ever did.

Harold's grandmother was Mary Ceta, also known as *Ihawastewin*, "Good Laughing Woman." She was one of the Hunkpapa Sioux who accompanied Sitting Bull into the safety of these hills after the Battle of Little Big Horn, and she married a former North-West Mounted Police officer, Jimmy H. Thomson. He'd been a good friend to the Sioux, and was given a proper Indian name, *Okalla.*

According to local lore, it was Harold's grandfather, Jimmy Thomson, who, at Six Mile Creek, shot the last buffalo in the Wood Mountain region. (Thomson's great grandson, Rory, turned twenty-two this summer and has been given his own Indian name, *Zincala,* or "Little Bird," in a ceremony out on the prairie.)

Mamie had met Good Laughing Woman and mentioned her in Wood Mountain stories with respect and a kind of awe, for Good Laughing Woman had become a local legend. She had eleven children and is remembered for her kindness and generosity although she steadfastly, and some would say stubbornly, refused to learn English. "She thought we should learn to speak Sioux," her great-grandson Rory tells me. "Maybe she was right, eh?"

Harold has the chiseled features of his ancestry, the same hospitable tendency toward strangers, and he's as much at ease with horses as he is with people.

"See the creek? Down there's a beaver dam. I tried to take my horse across there one day, and we fell into a bog. The horse was getting pulled down. He was in right up to his head. I thought we'd both drown. I tried to keep his head up, and I told him, 'I got you into this, old boy, and I'll get you out, or we'll go down together.'"

The dogs find a small slough and wade in up to their bellies and come out shaking ecstatically. Avoiding the beaver dam, we walk the horses through a meadow splashed with wildflowers—bluebells, pink yarrow, black-eyed susans, low-growing roses. There's a honey-scented breeze blowing off a field of fresh-cut clover, and cottony-looking clouds are building cumulus towers thousands of feet straight up into the pure cerulean blue of the biggest sky I've ever seen. Betty, using wire stretchers, has opened the gates. "I like fencing," she says. "Don't mind it at all—gives me time to think."

Slicker steps gingerly around the barbed wire as we head into a ditch along the road allowance, and there's a sickening crunch of breaking glass when his hoof lands on a beer bottle. "Some fool threw that out of a car," says my brother, "some fool who doesn't own a horse."

When I get off Slicker after an easy three-hour ride, during which he only once broke into a canter for about ten steps, I'm sunburned, windblown, mosquito bitten and my knees feel like they're made of jelly. "Now I know why you cowboys walk funny," I tell my brother, but I feel terrific. I think of Mamie racing bareback across these hills with her hair tucked up in her funny crocheted cap and her long black riding skirt billowing a little in the wind, and I know why she never wanted to leave.

:

At dusk I watch a ferruginous hawk on a fence post, watching me. He swivels his head halfway around his body, regards me solemnly with his peculiar hawkish scowl and then swivels back and looks toward the south hills, as though he's considering weighty matters. Distance and wind speed, maybe. He turns again, disgusted to find this wingless earthling still gawking at him. Fluffs his feathers, gives out a loud, sorrowful screech with that falling note at the end that makes a hawk's cry so melancholy. Flaps his great ruffled wings then, by way of preparing for takeoff, and glides into the sky, effortlessly, smoothly, not a feather twitching. He circles once, gives his sharp hawk screech and sails away, southward over the hills.

In a minimalist landscape, uncluttered by tall buildings or even tall trees, the sky takes up more room than I remembered. It's enormous, and it changes from moment to moment as the wind blows the clouds around, rearranging them, now fluffy, cumulus piles, now wispy, nimbostratus veils trailing across the blue. All day long they keep moving, the sky keeps changing, and as evening comes sky-watchers like me take to the hilltops.

You could drown in a prairie sunset. When the color washes across all that sky—yellow, gold, orange, red, sometimes slipping into halftones of pink and mauve—it lights up the tops of the hills, and the tops of the shelterbelt trees, so they glow, briefly, like so many candles. I used to think we could catch up with the sunset. Heading west in the back of Dad's Ford, driving home from Sunday dinner at Aunt Roma's, I silently willed him to go faster: *Step on the gas, Dad. Drive right into all that light.*

Mamie was a sunset watcher too, and she used to tell me, *Shush now, let's be really quiet,* as though she were expecting some celestial choir to burst into song at any minute. My mother, Pearl, who graduated from a Brownie Starflash to a Canon Sureshot, took roll after roll of sunset slides, most of them with two or three grain elevators silhouetted against the spectacular hues.

After dark the stars take over. On a clear night I have an overwhelming urge to lay on my back and stare up at them, and suddenly it comes to mind that Mamie did this too. She never told me about it, but here, now, I'm certain of it. On the cosmic clock—the one that makes the allotted human span hardly worth mentioning—time pretends to stand still, and for this briefest possible fragment, this mere splinter of time in the cold, white light of Mamie's stars, I can almost believe that it does.

I fall asleep listening to an owl hoot. Just after three in the morning, the dogs wake me. Every dog on the farm is howling, and then, above the racket, I hear the other sound, the high, lonesome wail coming from the hills. Coyotes. *Yip, yip, yip-awoo.* They sing in perfect cadence, high and wild and beautiful, *yipyipyip-awoooo . . .* There's more than one singer out there, so the wail becomes a sort of round, and in my mind's eye I can see the pack, silvery in the early dawn, sitting on lean haunches, eyes nearly closed, heads flung back, jaws pointed at the waning moon.

There's no middle ground with a coyote's howl. You either love its haunting quality, or it makes your blood run cold. For the farm dogs maybe it's a reminder of lost freedom, of running with a pack, when no man was their master.

Somebody yells at the dogs to shut up, and they're reduced to a couple of low growls, then obedient silence. Away out there in the hills, the coyotes keep on singing because nobody tells a coyote to shut up.

from **old coyote hunting man**

when Mattie gives birth to coydogs
he kills all seven
breaks their necks
the same way a coyote fells a sheep
he says
> *that will teach the bitch*
> *running with coyotes at night*

next day Mattie leaves
she runs coyotes in daylight
—*Thelma Poirier,* Grasslands

The next day, an antelope appears from nowhere, running in a fenced field, racing our car. It's a small, compact animal, all grace and beauty, strongly muscled hindquarters, fragile-looking forelegs, running lightly, as though it had springs in its feet. I can clearly see the brown and cream markings of the coat, the gentle curvature of the horns, the big eyes. There's another fence coming up, doubtless its barbed wire, and the long-legged runner is heading straight for it.

"Stop," I yell, either to the antelope or to Ed, my patient husband, who has been driving prairie backroads since he was a kid, and wouldn't know what slow down meant. So again I yell, "Stop, dammit!" certain that we're about to cause a tragedy. But the antelope has seen more barbed wire fences than I have, and at the last possible second, it ducks. Slips *under* the fence, and springs across the road in front of us, heading off into open pasture.

"Yeah, they do that all the time. An antelope is supple, and he's smart. He'll go *under* the fence every time," Harold Thomson, who knows these things, tells me later. "Not like a deer—a deer will jump clean over it, and then it'll run right into your car."

Moving across the prairie with the antelope is the ever-present wind. Aunt Violet remembers: "We'd been over to the corral for the branding, and the clouds moved in, all yellow and brown, rolling so's you could almost reach up and touch them. Well sir, this wind come along so fast it picked up the big Quonset and smacked it against the house—just slivered it."

In July the wind speed in the grasslands averages twelve miles an hour, and has reached as high as eighty.

I've always wondered why the wind that blows so long and strong across these south Saskatchewan drylands doesn't have it's own name. Other, less impressive winds have names. There's the *mistral*, the wind that blows down from the Alps into southern France for one hundred days a year, the wind that drives people mad. And the *tramontane*, the cold wind that blows across the Italian border, traveling northeast into France. There are the *sirocco*, the two Italian winds that are always warm, one carrying rain, the other carrying dust from the southern deserts. There's the *simoom* blowing hot and dry off the Sahara, rising suddenly, lasting ten minutes or ten days, according to the overheating of the sand.

There are the more obscure local winds of the African deserts—the *khamsin* that blows off the Sahara into Egypt every spring for fifty days in a row, and the *harmattan,* the perfidious winter wind blowing west southwest from the same desert to the African coast, avoided by pilots who know its turbulent habits and its strength. There's the *rifi,* named for the mountainous region of the northern coast of Morocco, and the *aajej* of southern Morocco— dry, sandy winds, these.

There are the Asian *monsoons* that blow off the ocean during summer and onto it during winter. There's the *Santa Ana,* the wind that turns California into a torch each summer, burning hundreds of millions of dollars worth of real estate. And there's the warm winter wind we call a *chinook,* blowing down from the Alberta Rockies, warming up one degree for every 180 feet or so that it descends, traveling east, turning a February day in Calgary or Lethbridge or Eastend into a sudden, false spring, leaving as fast as it came. The same sort of wind blowing warmly off the Alps is called a *foehn.*

But apart from this, the prairie wind has no name. It has been described often enough, heaven knows. The wayward wind. The restless wind. The four winds. *They call the wind Mariah. . . .* And so forth.

It seems to me this prairie wind should have its own name and its own book. Maybe there isn't a word in English that would serve as an adequate descriptor. How to convey the searing heat and the brutal cold this wind carries around with it, each in its own season? How to describe the noise? The singing and yowling and crying and howling. Animal sounds, human sounds, for this prairie wind is a clever mimic, able to laugh and cry in the same breath.

The beating, the pushing and tearing, the shredding of leaves, the tattering of school yard flags, the shoving at your back.

The bending.

One thing you learn early on the prairies is to bend with the wind. Bend with it just like the grass does. Those things it can't bend, the wind with no name will break.

Prairie people may have started out with different languages, customs and beliefs, even different looks, but the prairie, its huge scale of sky and wind, has buffed the sharp edges off their differences, given them a new identity with their own language, customs, and beliefs, and even in subtle ways their own look.

I see other differences, always have, and for my part I like prairie people's natural reserve, the gentle courtesy I still find among them, the willingness to extend a helping hand when the chips are down. Hospitality comes naturally here, and the tough exterior of the prairie farmer is cushioned by a certain generosity of spirit that is seldom far below the surface. Of all things that set them apart, what strikes me most is the way in which the traditional pessimism of prairie people, marked by those who have lost and lost again, is tempered by eternal, unquenchable hope.

CHAPTER 4

And Now, the News: Summer 1996

A T THE ENTRANCE TO THE WEST Block of the Grasslands Park sits Val Marie, a village where tall cottonwoods blow in the wind and the Frenchman River, here reduced to a narrow, muddy creek, meanders through. Like a number of other prairie villages that have seen better days, Val Marie's claim to fame is an NHL hockey star, and a billboard announces Val Marie, Home of Bryan Trottier .

A pot of leggy purple petunias sits near the open doorway of Rusty's Cafe, leaves already wilting in the morning sun. Inside are three booths along the north wall, and four or five tables have been pushed together down the middle in the manner of small-town restaurants whose most loyal and frequent clients are the morning koffee klatch. At 10:30 on a Wednesday morning, the regulars are gathering.

Rusty, a gray-haired woman of indeterminate age, is at her counter. Behind her, on top of a large fridge, a family photograph: three generations with Rusty in the middle. She brings toast and

coffee to our booth and makes a second trip with a screw-top pint
sealer of the type Mamie and Pearl used for canning fruit in the fall.
"You like homemade jam? I made 159 jars yesterday."

Where else but here, in the heart of the prairie, would anybody
make 159 jars of jam, let alone count them? It's good jam, and I can
taste rhubarb, saskatoons, strawberries and orange peel. It tastes of
childhood, three of us in the kitchen, with Pearl stirring big, slow
circles in the white enamel jam pot on the stove and Mamie in her
apron at the table, picking over another basket of saskatoons, telling
me to stop eating all the big ones and get sorting. We too counted
our jars when they'd been filled and wiped down for splashes. For a
prairie woman, there was something reassuring and beautiful about
all those jars. It was the sort of detail Mamie liked to record in her
Cash Book. *July 15, 1921, 159 jars of saskatoon jam*, she'd have written.

At the middle table, two men wearing baseball caps are joined
by a gray-haired woman addressed as Mary. A youngish guy just
back from holidays sports a white T-shirt with *Virgin Islands* stamped
on it. Somebody acknowledges the geography on his shirt, and he
makes a joke. "You know the definition of a virgin? Youngest girl in
kindergarten!" Tentative laughter from some around the table.

"The rear end went out of my truck yesterday. Vent plugged up."
This from Mary, who didn't laugh at the joke.

The next arrival, greeted as Doc, is a middle-aged East Indian
man wearing a white shirt and tie. Now that so many young Canadian doctors shun the long hours and relatively few amenities of general practice in rural areas, the void is often filled by offshore talent,
medical men and women who perhaps see a stint in rural
Saskatchewan as a bit of exotica, an adventure on a latter-day frontier.
So here is Doc, whose British accent and perfect diction attest to good
boarding schools and an education abroad. His practice is elsewhere
in some other slightly larger town, but he holds occasional office

hours in Val Marie. He takes the chair at the head of the table. "You know the definition of stress, don't you? It is the denial of illness."

Everybody laughs at Doc's joke, and Mary laughs hardest, says, "That's a good one."

By 10:45 there are seven at the center table. One of the men gets up and pours a round of coffee, then strolls over to our booth and refills our cups. "Might as well, seein' as I'm up."

When I pay the bill, Rusty herself deposits the money in a cash register, an older model propped up with soup cans bearing yellowed labels. I ask how long she's been in business.

"Fourteen in the hotel next door. Thirty years in this joint. Guess I'll stay."

Driving Highway 18 east from Val Marie, heading toward the Mankota turnoff, a small herd of pronghorn antelope grazing in a field. They look up as we pass, momentarily curious, and go right back to cropping grass. We meet five pickup trucks for every car, and every driver waves. In spite of the out-of-province plates, it's assumed that every vehicle down here is driven by a friend, relative or acquaintance, or a stranger with no evil motives, and the courtesy of a wave is extended.

Just before the turnoff, where half a dozen Hereford steers are loose in a ditch, a red pickup screeches to a stop. The passenger is a little guy, maybe ten years old. The driver, so short that he must have been sitting on a telephone book to see over the steering wheel, can't be a day over ten. We watch as they round up the recalcitrant livestock, herd the protesting animals over the downed wire fence and quickly fix it. They get back in the truck and the driver waves as he turns the truck around on the road and drives away. My husband, returning the wave, smiles to himself. So I ask him, "How old were you when you started driving your dad's truck?" He gives me a typical prairie answer: "Oh, about ten."

A radio station plays country and western music interspersed with public service announcements and a farm news program. A commentator hotly defends the cattle industry and promotes the eating of beef: "Did you know that cabbage has sixty times as much hormones in it as beef? Maybe that's why so many vegetarians are hormonally challenged."

More country music, then a local news broadcast, leading with an item from the town of Kindersley: "Here's a real snake-in-the-grass story. Seems there's a three-meter Mexican tree boa on the loose. That's about six feet of snake, folks. He eats small mammals, so keep an eye on your cats." Later in the week, the unfortunate reptile is discovered dead in somebody's stove. A second snake, seemingly a companion of the first, is apprehended in someone's trailer. The Kindersley town council immediately passes a bylaw making it illegal to own or possess exotic snakes on pain of a five-hundred-dollar fine. Radio commentators declare Kindersley to be a snake-free zone.

At the Mankota turnoff we head south on a gravel grid road, watching for the marker to the West Block of the Grasslands. Many of the metal road signs have round holes in them from a shotgun or maybe a rifle aimed from a passing truck.

The seventeen-mile dirt road that winds through the park is okay if it doesn't rain. A brochure warns bluntly, "When it starts to rain, leave quickly, or you may have to stay until the road dries out." The same brochure also points out that there is no drinking water in the park, that sturdy boots are advised against cactus spines, that rattlesnakes should not be disturbed and that binoculars are handy, the best times for wildlife viewing being dawn and dusk. At high noon, citizens of the Grasslands know enough to stay in the cool of their underground burrows or hunker down in whatever shade they can find.

Soon the narrow road winds downward off the tabletop prairie into the mile-wide valley gouged out by the Frenchman River. It seems little more than a stream, yet the strength and size this river once had can be judged by the original banks, rising 300 to 500 feet on either side of the valley floor. This west and larger block of the Grasslands is part of the proposed 350 square miles that it will one day become as it is gradually returned to native prairie.

Water is the key to survival in this part of the prairies, but it's hard to come by and harder to hang onto. Even though rainfall averages around twelve inches of rain per year, the sun and wind evaporate it so fast that desert conditions prevail. During the summer months, tornadoes race through these uninhabited areas, daytime updrafts produce towering thunderheads and fierce thunder and lightning rolls across the land at night, unnoticed except for the Doppler radar that tracks such things.

A week later, on a grid road between Rockglen and Wood Mountain, a strong west wind pushes the waving foxtails nearly flat, sends clouds scudding across the open sky, bends the few trees. These willow and poplar trees, as well as the caragana bushes are heavy rooters that go deep enough to anchor against the tugging of the wind, trees that find water when the rains don't come. The car shakes in the wind.

A highway sign notes that we're passing Killdeer, a hamlet so thoroughly hidden among the hills that it's not visible from the road. Noticing railway ties stacked beside the sign, I remember something I heard yesterday, a casual remark over a cup of coffee in somebody's living room: "They're taking the railway out between Rockglen and Killdeer."

Later, I sit for hours with a slender green coil-backed book, *They Came to Wood Mountain*, published in 1967 by the local historical society, and I read part of the Killdeer story, the good and hopeful part, the sky-is-the-limit part familiar to so many prairie people. Once upon a time Killdeer was a busy little hamlet providing services to the local farmers who lived in the surrounding hills, and for a while there was a farm almost every mile. The hamlet got its own post office in 1919. The CPR built a branch line, and soon there was a modest building boom—two grain elevators, Charlie Weed's cafe, Van Ripley's general store, Lloyd Morrison's barbershop and Bert Colbo's lumberyard. The women of the community formed a homemaker's club, and they met regularly, repeating their creed and their motto—For Home and Country—and after a short business meeting they'd work on a project and have cake and coffee. They were community workers, these women. Tireless fundraisers, educators, knitters of socks, makers of baby diapers, holders of countless bazaars, caterers of weddings. Although the menfolk might have made light of their activities, referring to their meetings as hen parties or gabfests, it was these women who civilized a little burg on a frontier. While it existed, they gave it a certain quality of life.

Killdeer suffered along with everybody else in the thirties, but it did survive, and for a couple of decades afterward it bumped along nicely. Its demise was a gradual thing, a process all too familiar to villages and hamlets throughout this southern prairie, where small communities continue to shrink and disappear. As Killdeer's children grew up and moved away, and then decided in the interests of making a living not to move back, the hamlet began to take on a lean and hungry look. Still, there were the few businesses, and the elevators with their resident grain buyers, always a good sign on the prairies.

Then the farmers started getting out of straight cereal grains. Monoculture cereal crops are a bad idea, the government said, and local farmers had to admit, albeit reluctantly, that for once the government was right. There was better money in oilseed crops, canola and sunola. They were encouraged to diversify. In retrospect that may have been the thing that sealed Killdeer's fate.

A man in his early seventies, who once did a short stint as a grain buyer before moving to Killdeer and farming tells me, "It started to go downhill when farmers started contracting everything they grew, canola and such, to big companies. Them big outfits sent in their own trucks, eh? No more need for the elevators."

There's an edge of nostalgia in his voice. Oh yes, the elevators—prairie sentinels, people called them. One every ten miles in his day, sometimes closer than that. Pool, National, Parrish and Heimbeker, Federal, Pioneer, United Grain Growers. Big companies, every one of them. Sometimes a town would have six or eight elevators lined up along the railway tracks. It made the town proud too. Gave it status.

For himself, well, his land's rented to a young fella who farms nine quarters. Does it all by computer, would you believe? Three winters ago, he and the wife moved into Assiniboia. Closed up the old house. Neither of his boys wanted to farm, and he figures it's just as well.

Without the elevator families in Killdeer and the business the elevators generated, there was less need for a cafe and a store and certainly nothing as effete as a barbershop, not with everybody driving to Rockglen or even Assiniboia for every little thing now that the roads are paved. And without the elevators, what use was a branch line railway?

In late August I call the Rural Municipality of Poplar Valley, of which Killdeer is a part, and the reeve, Mr. Bell, comes on the line. I ask if he can tell me the exact population of Killdeer.

Reeve Bell asks who wants to know.

I tell him my name, that I'm researching a book, that all I want is a current figure. So how many people still live in Killdeer?

He pauses, sighs, and finally says, "Oh, about four people and five dogs, I guess."

Already, the roadbed is weedy where it curves away into the hills.

Items of Interest

In Mamie's day, one Canadian farmer could produce enough food to feed seven to ten people. Now, one farmer can produce enough for ninety people. Many of the farmer's neighbors have left, but the operation is bigger, more specialized, and costs are much higher while profit margins are lower.

In 1901 Canada's population was 5.3 million, and 62 percent were farmers. Today, that figure has dropped to 3 percent. The year Mamie left the Wood Mountain farm, 15 percent of the average farm's production went onto the family table. Now, .5 percent goes on the family table, and 99.5 percent of production is sold off the farm.

The year Mamie died, 141 small towns and villages in Saskatchewan were still considered viable. That number has dwindled as rural schools closed and the infrastructure continued to improve, whisking rural people to larger centers for shopping, schools and medical care. From 1951–1971, 2,750 rural schools were closed in Saskatchewan. During the same period, the miles of paved highways jumped from 750 to 10,000.

And so it goes.

At the Valley City Motel in Rockglen, an envelope is taped to the office door with my name and room number. In the envelope, a key. Management has gone shopping to Assiniboia and won't be back until late. I should let myself in.

I hadn't been near Rockglen for at least thirty years and wondered if it too would be disappearing into the prairie landscape. It was a relief to find the village holding its own, however tenuously. The windbreaks have grown up, and in a wet year like this the tall swaying poplars give the town a lush look. The few old houses that stand empty are balanced by a street of new ones, and at this time of day, approaching sunset, the western hills catch the light and hold it, momentarily bathing Rockglen in gold.

There's a certain hopeful pride here. In the heart of town, one street leads downhill into a tidy business district, where three pickup trucks and a car are parked in front of the Rockglen Branch, Palliser Regional Library. A sign on the New Horizons Senior Citizens Drop-In Centre announces that anybody over forty is welcome, and in the Uptown Hair Design next door, two women are getting their hair done. A few doors away, the Short 'n' Sassy has closed, its sign painted over. There's a liquor vendor, a Sears mail order, a confectionery and bus station, and a big community hall. But the new-looking hospital has become the Grassland Health Centre. Those in need of a doctor drive to Assiniboia or Moose Jaw, and the CPR station has become a museum. When I try to visit during advertised open hours, it's closed.

The place for breakfast is Lou's, a long, windowless room in the basement of Cousin's Hotel, on the windy west end of Centre Street. The decor is half knotty pine, half rough white plaster, with silk greenery reflected in decorative mirrors. A bulletin board advertises goods and services: a farrier service (hot, cold or corrective shoeing and trimming), custom baling, an upcoming bridal shower. Somebody has a kitchen suite for sale. There's a lost dog; an unspecified reward is offered. A small white mongrel grins from a laser photo.

The waitress, automatically pouring coffee from a Pyrex pot, says she'll bring menus right away. The place mats in Lou's are laminated menus, and I tap a finger on mine by way of inquiry: "Isn't this the menu?"

"You *wish*," she says and points to the prices.

T-bone steak, $1.75

Coffee, tea, 5¢ extra

The placemat menu dates from an earlier incarnation, Ken's Cafe, 1960. After Mamie's time, but I should remember it. I likely drank a cup of that five-cent tea with my mother at least once.

Two tables are occupied this morning. All the customers are seniors, probably nearer eighty than sixty. All the men wear ball caps with logos on them, Co-op Oil or Pool, which marks them as farmers. Four men and a woman sit at the first table, having pulled up an extra chair. Two women occupy the next table and are soon joined by the gray-haired cook, who comes in from her kitchen, carrying her personal coffee mug. Twice during breakfast young business types breeze in, pass the time of day over a fast coffee and leave, but the seniors stay on and on.

The tables talk back and forth, moving in and out of one another's conversations by raising their voices half a notch or so while simultaneously maintaining their own topics. It's like a club with memberships that go back to Rockglen's youth, so now in their retirement, when they can afford the time and the price of the coffee, why not the local cafe?

This morning they discuss the weather (bad), the crops (not bad, considering the weather) and the Boundary Commission trail ride that went through town last night.

"Nice horses. Percherons. Clydes. No more cowboy hats and boots, though. Just caps and runners now." This from a man wearing a cap with a green and white Co-op Oil logo. This morning in Lou's Cafe, there's not a Stetson or a Plimsoll coat in sight. I make a note to ask my aunt: Does this mean that greenhorns no longer affect western dress while playing cowboy?

A man at the first table mentions the team of smart little buckskins he saw pulling one of the wagons: "Them buckskins got a lot of heart."

There's muttered agreement on the buckskins, but a woman at table two interjects, shooting down the wagon idea. "I don't care to see no more wagons. Seen enough of them years ago. Eleven miles into town, eleven miles back." She makes a derisive hissing sound, whistling through her teeth, and I want to introduce myself, ask her about those long miles and the wagon, but she changes the subject. "I'm not sure I'm gonna get any cucumbers this year."

From the horse enthusiast at table one, a touch of prairie optimism: "Sure you will if it don't hail no more or freeze." Weather, ever capricious and sneaky, is the butt of a hundred prairie jokes. This one gets a big laugh. The waitress saunters over to his table to refill his cup, and he favors her with a grin. "Hell, I figured I was gonna die of thirst before you got here with that."

Apropos of nothing, he asks a riddle, and oddly enough, it's the same riddle I heard in Val Marie—the stress riddle—but the answer is different: "What's the definition of stress?" General muttering, but nobody volunteers an answer. "Ten thousand flies and you can't find the swatter!"

Talk turns to dogs. Somebody's dog barked all night, but a reasonable excuse is offered—"Must have been coyotes close to town." The dog in question belongs to somebody at the table, and the majority opinion is that it's young and therefore naturally yappy, but it has potential. This is verified by the owner, who speaks on its behalf.

"Got two gophers already. One yesterday, one the day before. Gonna be a damn good dog."

Driving toward Wood Mountain, still referred to by a few old-timers as the new town to distinguish it from the earlier established North-West Mounted Police post of the same name, I can see what drew people to it. Nestled among rolling hills with poplars growing here and there, a busy farming district all around it and the promise of a railway, it's the sort of place where an enterprising people might very well build themselves a fine and prosperous town. When the railway came through, Wood Mountain's future seemed assured. Both stores from the post pulled up stakes and moved here. The town was surveyed in 1927 and incorporated in 1930.

Maybe its timing was bad, being born just as the surrounding prairie was hit by a long and disastrous drought, and the land began to take its toll on those who had broken it, Mamie's family among them.

Once again I'm lost in the green book *They Came to Wood Mountain,* looking for clues. Wood Mountain tried hard. By the time it was an official town, it had already sent some of its young men to war. Two to the Boer War, twenty-one to the First World War. A few years more and over one hundred men would leave the little community to fight in the Second World War. Many, too many by far from this and from other towns across the prairies, would not come back.

Excerpts from the early council minutes, Village of Wood Mountain, show it to have started life as a busy, thriving farm community serving a large trading district. In my imagination, I see the community as it was, with much coming and going of horses and vehicles along the busy main street, women shopping, men doing farm errands for machinery or livestock, people stopping to pass the time of day, for there were few strangers here. Wood Mountain had four grain elevators, a Canadian Pacific Railway station, a drayman to deliver freight from the station, a post office, a livery stable and three lumberyards. Housewives had a choice of two general merchants, three butcher shops and a drugstore. A beer and wine store, a poolroom, a barbershop, a shoemaker and harness shop, two farm implement agencies and a garage made it worthwhile for the menfolk to come into town and linger awhile. Jimmie Hoy and Charlie Soo both had hotels and Hoy also ran a cafe.

In September 1930, the garbage that always follows on the heels of human settlement was beginning to pile up, so two acres of land at thirty-five dollars per acre were purchased from Costa Radu for a nuisance ground. In October, Dr. Woods of Limerick was appointed medical health officer at fifty dollars per annum.

By 1931 the temper of the prairie was beginning to cause considerable pain in the town, washing in from the suffering farms that surrounded it. According to the town minutes for August, men who applied for social assistance, referred to as relief, were to work on the village streets. For this they would be paid twenty-five cents per hour.

In May, two streetlights were erected. They were especially welcomed by local farmers, who used them as hitching posts.

In March of the following year, George Moisiuk was paid the sum of six dollars to wreck the old tannery building. In June a bylaw forbade ranchers to let their livestock run at large in the village. But there was not so much livestock as there had been, and in November the lumber from the recently demolished tannery was used to build a curling rink.

In April 1939 the old Walberg building was repaired for use as a village hall. More pretentious folk might have called it a town hall, or even the council chambers, but Wood Mountain called it like it was: a hall in a village. Times began to get better, and the people could breathe easy again.

In October 1940 the local homemakers' club was granted use of the hall for a handicraft course. In December Jack Moneo applied to rent the hall so he could show motion pictures, and in February the local young people's club was given free use of the hall, but had to supply their own light and fuel and were firmly cautioned that they'd be responsible for any damages.

In April, council discussed the necessity of installing hitching racks for farmers' horses.

In 1949 two land purchases are worth noting, if only for what they say about the natural course of a community's life: the first was for a playground; the second was for a cemetery.

By the fifties there were big changes in the new town. An RCMP detachment and a telephone office had been added. Three garages and a service station were doing a good business with the farmers in the surrounding district, and there was a dairy. In February 1956 the Saskatchewan Power Corporation took over village lighting.

With the coming of the sixties, a thin veil of prosperity lay across Wood Mountain. Cars had long ago replaced the horse as transportation, and in October 1962 the old livery barn was sold and removed from the village. In April 1964 a new curling rink was built under a winter works program. In February, Saskatchewan Government Telephones took over the rural telephones for Wood Mountain and Fir Mountain.

But within a decade Wood Mountain began feeling the stress of a changing world. Although there were still two cafes, two general stores, two garages, two grain elevators and a hotel, business was down, and the new town was shrinking visibly. The population of small farms on which the town depended for its existence could no longer make a living by conventional methods, and their children would not or could not stay on the land.

Reading the green book, I'm reminded that in another time and another place, the ancestors of these same farmers went through a similar crisis. Unable to make a living on the land available to them, unable to find work, they had left their villages in great numbers—Germans, Poles, Czechs and Slovaks, Rumanians, Ruthenians and Galicians, Brits, Swedes and, yes, Americans. As they left for the new world some of their home villages dwindled, and others became enclaves of the very old, and a few, like Magdalena's Schanau Rhinebirn in Bavaria, just disappeared from the map.

On what was likely called Main Street, a block of false-front buildings, one still bearing the hotel sign, has been boarded up. The town is quiet today. An hour goes by and nothing happens. The wind blows and somewhere a tin sign bangs and clangs, but in that hour, no dog, human or vehicle ventures into the street.

The mayor is out in the yard when I phone, but his wife answers my questions. She tells me the population stands at forty-eight, but she wants to know why I'm asking and hastens to assure me in a half-worried voice that it's really much higher than that when you consider the trading area with dozens of farms. She adds firmly that it's a lovely community, really friendly, and it has a lot of history.

And all of this is true. In fact, the hills around Wood Mountain hold more than their share of creative people, a community of skilled artists, writers and poets who have a depth of understanding for this land and its people that goes far beyond the usual. The town has a historical society, a 4-H Club, a rodeo committee, and its annual rodeo and stampede, which has been a howling success for 106 years running, draws huge crowds from all over the south and across the line.

But the hard fact is that these days in Wood Mountain, you can't send your kids to a local school, can't see a doctor or buy a newspaper. You can't buy groceries although there's still a gas station. The only new-looking building in town is the municipal office which shares space with the post office in the other half, and in the time-honored tradition of small prairie towns, you can pick up your mail and do a little socializing at the same time. But you can't see a movie or a play or order a pizza although you can rent a video at the local bar and grill. There's a small library that opens for a few hours a week. If you need a birthday gift or a postcard, one of the houses on Main Street has been turned into a souvenir shop, handling a small selection of local crafts. The pretty white church is much the worse for wear and in need of paint, but nobody bothers anymore. Services are held, but not every Sunday. There's no resident clergy, either Protestant or Roman Catholic. The two bright orange Pioneer elevators are on somebody's hit list for demolition.

At least one business is alive and well and booming in Wood

Mountain. If you make a right turn at the north end of Main Street, you'll find the old curling rink. Although nobody floods the ice anymore, and the great international war cry of *Sweep, SWEEP* hasn't been heard for some time, the rink serves a purpose—the Wood Mountain Bar and Grill is attached it.

On the Grill's storm porch, a big yellow dog stirs himself and moves out of the way so we can open the door. It's noon and the air in the coffee shop is heavy with smoke from a dozen cigarettes and a short-order grill, fuming with burgers, fries, Denvers. Every booth is full, but just beyond this room, just past the amazingly lifelike wood carving of a bear standing on its hind legs is a larger dining room. I have an impression of parties past and future, and of dancing if they push back the tables and turn up the music. A black leatherette bar stands in one corner of the room, and a selection of rentable videos runs along the end, near a large television set and a pile of stacking chairs. Pictures are scattered around the walls at varying heights: Indian chief, horse, Indian maiden, another horse. Someone has hung up an old tractor seat, the metal kind with holes in it for ventilation. A big portable table fan and a second fan in the ceiling attest to the frequent hot weather this place gets in July.

But since when can you trust the weather down here? On this July day the wind howls and pushes at the Quonset structure, tugs at the storm porch, reminds us that the next season to come is fall, and in this country a killing frost has been known to arrive as early as August 7.

Marcelle Robichaud, still wearing the blue cap he had on when he came to work this morning, is everywhere at once, pouring coffee, taking orders, cooking, passing the time of day with customers in both rooms, answering the phone. If you call the number for the town of Wood Mountain, as advertised in a tourist guide to the area, the phone will ring right here, and Marcelle will probably answer.

A couple of people look vaguely familiar, and a tall Indian with chiseled features and a leathery face joins the coffee drinkers in one booth. Beneath a black Stetson, dark braids hang to his shoulders.

"Lots of people in the park yet?" he asks. It's the weekend of the stampede, the three day event that has been part of my family mythology for as long as I can remember, and the biggest event of the year here for much longer than that.

"Yeah, I imagine it'll start to fill up about now," comes a reply.

"Great weather for it." Laughter.

Aunt Violet said this yesterday: "We never missed a rodeo, Leonard and I." My mother, forty years ago, said this: "The rodeo was the biggest event of the year. We'd take a picnic and spend a whole day." Mamie, correcting my mother, said this: "We always called it the Sports. Not the rodeo; the Sports."

We settle in the second room, and when a customer at the next table borrows the catsup we trade greetings, prairie style, opening with the weather.

"Seems like there's been a lot of rain around here this year," I offer.

"Yeah, but it's too late for some of the hay. Seems like there's always something, don't it?"

He's an older man, about my father's age. He leans forward and introduces himself, and when I tell him my name a light goes on in his face.

"I was one of your uncle's best friends. Hell, I was named after him."

I mutter sympathetically about the hay crop, and after a while I carefully mention that some people I've talked to say this land would have been better left to grass, not broken up for farming.

Yeah, some of it should have been left to grass. No doubt about that. But the bottoms had good land. Real good. Those people had to make a living, so they broke up the land. What else could they do? Now, trying to farm the hillsides like some of them do, pulling that damn big machinery around, summer fallowing it to death—that's plain crazy.

I tell him I've heard a range ecologist refer to the same practice as *recreational tillage.* He smiles at that, agrees that summer fallow isn't the best way to deal with this light, blowy soil. Some local farmers use zero till now—stubble left on the ground, weeds killed by an application of biodegradable weed killer, and seeding is done with an air drill. The new crop grows right up through the old roots and remaining straw, which serve as a sort of mulch to hold the soil in place.

But I've seen a lot of summer fallow in the area, and what do you do in a dry year, I ask. What do you do if it starts to blow?

"You hide!" He laughs, the raspy laugh of a heavy smoker, pushes his Saskatchewan Wheat Pool cap back on his head, leans forward in his chair for emphasis. "I was through lots of that in the fifties. My dad before me in the thirties."

Strange things happen on these prairies, where wind, lack of rain and people's stewardship of the land all factor into a kind of precarious balancing act. I ask about Old Wives Lake, the huge body of water Mamie described as the big, salty lake she had passed on her journey to Wood Mountain. When it was full, this catch basin of salty water covered 120 square miles, and was the fourth largest saline lake in North America. Since the summer of 1988, it's been almost empty—a salty mud flat that blew up poisonous clouds of sulfurous dust that first summer and has since become a bed for certain salt-loving weeds and poisonous algae. Was it true that it had dried up once before, during the thirties and made a comeback? He thinks so though he's not certain, and most of the people who would know are dead, or gone from the district.

Not much reason to go there anyway. Never was. It's a lonely place, spooky even. Always been salty, and since that summer of 1988, when the rains didn't come, it's sure enough been dry a lot of the time.

"If you ask me, I'd say farming's about finished. No fun anymore. Young people leaving, towns dying . . . Nobody's thrown a rock in this curling rink for fifteen, maybe sixteen years."

Why are the young people leaving? He shrugs, stubbing out a cigarette, giving me one of those prairie answers.

"Can't afford to farm. These days, a farmer's gotta have too much land. Machinery costs a fortune. You take one of them big fifty-foot cultivators like they use now—you're looking at big bucks. Interest is too damn high. Then you got your fuel, your fertilizers, your weed spray. The wives are all working off the farm, trying to help pay the bills. . . . Another ten years and this'll be a desolate place. Won't be nobody left to farm."

Although Mamie had once worked off the farm, during her brief tenure as a cook on an American ranch, farm women of her generation were not expected to work away from their home turf. But, as two wars took men out of the workforce and the devastating effects of the dirty thirties further eroded tradition roles of women, the possibility of a second wage became increasingly attractive.

Between 1941 and 1991, costs of land and equipment spiralled and the percentage of women who worked off the farm doubled. Roughly 66 percent of farm spouses now work off the farm, generating approximately 33 percent of the operating revenues.

But for the moment, there are those who are so tied to this land and its ways that they can't imagine anything else. People like Dwight and Karen Forwood, who own the Bar F, a small ranch in the hills southeast of Wood Mountain. The Forwood family has been here since 1916. Dwight spent eight years in Toronto, where he met Karen, but he belonged here, and he wanted to come home. She's lived on these one thousand acres for twenty-four years now, and it's her home too. Still, this idyllic-sounding life in the peaceful hills of Palliser's Triangle is no easy row to hoe, not for Karen, not for her family. Three days a week, she drives forty miles into Assiniboia to her job in a senior's lodge and forty miles back. "It's no problem in the summer, but the winter's can be bad. The roads can get real slippery; a blizzard comes up fast. . . ."

A couple of summers ago, she opened a bed and breakfast in the house, named it after the ranch: The Bar F Bed and Breakfast. Though she wasn't home until late last night, she's up with the birds this morning, feeding dogs, slicing watermelon, making coffee and waffles, being sociable with the strangers at her table.

"Beautiful day for the Stampede, but I wish it would rain. Our hay crop is already toast," she tells me, ladling waffle batter into the iron.

Dwight and Karen's three children are grown, and one son is in college in Winnipeg. A daughter, Allison, wants a career as a veterinary technician. She'll be leaving for agricultural college in the fall, and Karen misses her already.

The oldest son is here, working on the ranch. Like his father he sits on the rodeo committee. He'll likely take over and could probably do it now, but Dwight is barely fifty, and for a man who loves his land, fifty-something is a long way from retirement. What happens when a son is old enough to take the reins, and a father isn't ready to move on? It can get hurtful, this generational war. Mamie knew about it, as did almost every woman who lived down here and watched her sons grow up, so proud to be like Dad, until the day they want him out of the way.

But these days the inevitable struggle when the torch is passed has become the lesser of two evils. Father and son will work it out.

The important thing is to keep the land in the family. Keep the ranch up and running.

Watching Karen bustle around her kitchen, I wonder: What if none of the kids had wanted to stay? Would some big foreign corporation have picked up their one thousand acres, turned it into some sort of factory farm, boarded up this pretty house and left it empty, like so many down here? Like Mamie's was, for so many years. Karen has thought long and hard about what's happening to the family farms here and elsewhere, and she doesn't much like what she's thinking.

"When these big corporate farms take over, where will the young farmers come from? You can't suddenly teach somebody to be a farmer. It comes from being born into it. Our kids were born into it, grew up handling stock, knowing about farm machinery. They dealt with all the problems too.

"Dwight gave each of them a calf—they got to pick their own. They raise it, worry about it, sell it. That was their money, all the money they had, and with it they had to buy their own clothes, so when they looked at those fancy designer jeans and shoes, they had to think real hard. . . . It made them responsible."

The big, sunny kitchen has recently been remodeled. Out the glass sliding doors I can see four dogs and a flower bed, and somewhere nearby are their cattle, a Japanese breed called Wagyu, noted for its marbling qualities. Dwight and the kids breeze through, grabbing a fast waffle, hurrying to get to the Stampede. Karen will follow later.

Watching her scoop waffle batter, I think about this place she has chosen. Last night, a hooting owl and the singing coyotes. Today, a 106-year-old festival whose participants celebrate by riding bulls and roping calves. It's about as different from the hustle of Yonge and Bloor as anything could be.

When I ask her if she ever wishes she was still in Toronto, she doesn't hesitate, not for a second.

"Never. This is my place now. I'm here to stay."

That's what Mamie said, once.

CHAPTER 5

The Wood Mountain Sports

HE POSTER ANNOUNCES THE 106TH
year of Canada's oldest continuous rodeo, the Wood Mountain
Stampede, July 12–14, 1996. Ever since I was a kid, listening to
Mamie and Pearl talk about this event, I've wanted to be here. Year
after year we'd planned to go, and something always interfered, so
we'd get there a week early or two weeks late. Today, the mystery will
be solved. I'll finally know what all the fuss was about.

Behind the corral, where dozens of horses are penned, riders are
exercising their mounts, walking them among the pickups and fifth
wheels and horse trailers that make up this temporary community.
There are dozens of tents from the Boundary Commission trail ride
that got in yesterday, but they're farther west, up near the hill with
Sitting Bull's marker. Now and then a horse up on the hill whinnies
loudly and is answered by a chorus of whinnying from the corral.
The wind carries the smell of dust and hot grease from the conces-
sion stand, which has been open all night, supplying the revelers with
fries and burgers, pizza and perogies. I order coffee and a hot dog.

"The band shut down around four, but we didn't even get a breather." This from the woman manning the deep fryer.

Midafternoon now. Sun high in a sky that is pure prairie blue, unbroken by even a wisp of cloud. Dust rising, stock being moved, cattle liners churning it up, bringing in the roping steers for tonight's performance. Slicker and Gus are tied to my brother's horse trailer, relaxed, lower lips hanging at half mast. Speck the dog naps under my folding chair. There's a Calcutta starting in the grandstand, and the auctioneer's voice comes singing down the wind, "Thirty-five, thirty-five, who'll a gimme forty. . . ."

And now to the cow pie contest, with its checkerboard grid marked on the grass behind the grandstand. Tickets cost five dollars, and the square on which the cow eventually deposits a pie is the lucky spot. A big-eyed Jersey has been elected, and she stands inside the little fence, bewildered, annoyed, occasionally bawling. One cowboy stops to have a word in her silken ear. "I got five bucks riding on this—you sure enough better crap on my square."

A local celebrity at the dunk tank competes with the Jersey for entertainment dollars. Soft ice cream is peddled from the back of one truck, fresh Okanagan cherries and T-shirts from another. There's a steak pit, and the beer garden is in a big, massively raftered Quonset with its north side open to the rodeo ring. A country and western band known as Bakers Field played until four this morning and will do it again tonight. For the benefit of athletically-inclined cowboys, signs are posted at regular intervals down the entire length of the Quonset: "Stay out of the rafters. Once, and you're out!"

The grandstand fills early, Stetsons and ball caps running about half and half—half cowboys, half farmers. A lot of people nod and grin, or say, "Hi, Howareya" because they figure they likely knew you as a child, or maybe your grandpa farmed next to their grandpa, and they should recognize you even though they don't. One old cowboy with a tracheotomy tube at his throat pauses to talk with friends. Pushing his ten-gallon hat back, he holds a finger over the tube and croaks painfully in the robot voice of a two-pack-a-day man who's paid the price. "Never missed a Sports for the last sixty-five years. Didn't see no reason to miss it now."

We clamber up to the top, so we're sitting right under the leafy canopy of freshly woven branches—caragana and the poplar known as quivering aspen. The gravel voice of a professional rodeo announcer introduces the essential clown, who rolls his barrel into the ring, shouts a couple of one-liners based on Bill Clinton's short-comings, and is suddenly drowned out as "O, Canada" blares forth. Caught off guard, the crowd gets uncertainly to its feet, ten-gallon hats and ball caps are yanked off and a cowgirl carrying a huge Cana-dian flag circles the ring at a full gallop with the scarlet maple leaf flowing obligingly and endearingly in the prairie wind.

The program lists the cowboys in each event and the mounts they've drawn for bareback, saddle bronco and bull riding get equal billing: Casino Strip and Terminator are saddle broncos; Maniac and Wild Bill are Brahma bulls.

Rodeo has never been a gentle sport, and there are those who refuse to call it a sport under any circumstances. Yet its events are so much a part of this place and these lives, that it loses the phony glitz of the big-money rodeos in major cities. Here, if anywhere, it belongs. I watch nervously, as I always have, wincing while a calf is roped by the hind leg and then the neck, so that having been jerked off its feet, it chokes until its tongue lolls and its eyes roll back. The announcer, cognizant of recent publicity, feels compelled to explain. "Now this might look a little harsh to some of you city folks, but if a calf needs doctorin', first thing you gotta do is choke it down."

The heavy horse pull is easier on the livestock. Bundles of shin-gles in ever-increasing weights are loaded on a skid, and a team of two draft horses attempts to pull them. The heavy money is on a team of delicate-looking Appaloosas, a small brown spotted pair, one evidently named Joey and a great favorite of the announcer. The crowd is with them—*They got heart, them little buggers*—and when they fail to budge the next load of shingles, heads shake and people mutter, *Aw, they coulda done that. . . .*

Now, thunder.

Thunder sounds different here. It reverberates through the hills like a kettle drum, rolling toward you from far away, coming closer and closer until you catch yourself looking up, you can't help it because you'd swear there was some visible force in collision right over your head. Some heavenly chariot race. Thor and his pals up there above the black-green, bruised-looking thunderheads that have come suddenly from nowhere. And just when you're certain the whole sky should be splitting, rending itself in two within the next millisecond, it rolls right on by and begins to fade back into the hills.

The rain on those few occasions when it does rain is seldom gentle. Like everything on the prairie it goes to extremes, and there you are, dry as a bone one minute, drenched the next.

Sitting in the stands, sheltered from the sun by our quivering leafy canopy of woven tree branches, nobody sees the storm coming until it's almost on top of us. We hear it, of course because on the prairies you can hear thunder for an hour without feeling a drop of rain.

When the clouds open and the rain comes down in buckets, straight and hard, the heavy horse pull is only half over, and down in the ring a pair of Clydesdales named Jack and Jim have been caught in the storm with their driver. Abandoning the bleachers, we make a mass beeline for the shelter of the open-sided Quonset where the beer flows and the music is loud.

Three young cowboys stand near us, faces tense. They competed yesterday in Selkirk, earlier today in Moosomin and now here in Wood Mountain, if the rain stops. They'll be at the dance tonight, and tomorrow they'll hit Elbow. Bulls and broncos are their events. Brahma bull riding pays pretty well, one of them says—when you win. Somebody bumps him, and he winces. He cracked a few ribs yesterday, but they're taped. He'll be okay to ride. Their faces are sunburned, and their necks, pale as milk under recent haircuts, look terribly vulnerable.

We all watch the storm, drinking cold beer, making small talk with strangers, feeling good because we're in a dry spot. Jacket crests identify their owner's place on the map: Great Falls or Medicine Hat or Alley's Palace in Glasgow, Montana. I'm fascinated by a woman's T-shirt, the back of which reads: *Stop breathin' on me. Yer rustin' my spurs.* Meanwhile the storm beats so hard on the tin roof that the music disappears into the persistent drumming rhythm of the rain.

Out there in the downpour a tall cowboy stands with Jack and Jim, holding their massive heads close to his, leaning his face against theirs, his Stetson angled so they all get a suggestion of shelter. Water pours off his hat brim like the downspout on an eaves trough. "I'll bet he's talkin' to them," says my brother, who'd happily be out there with them.

Ten minutes later, the rain quits and the sun comes out. Time for another beer, then back to the stands. In an hour the dust will be rising again. It takes more than a few drops of rain to stop a 106-year-old rodeo.

Epilogue:
1997

The body repeats the landscape. They are the source of each other,
and create each other. We are marked by the seasonal body of earth,
by the terrible migrations of people, by the swift turn of the century.
—MERIDEL LE SUEUR, *The Ancient People and the Newly Come*

I WONDER ABOUT THIS. IS IT THE relentless effort of our ancestors or blind luck or fate that molds us and our lives and the very land we stand on? Some would say it's none of these. Instead, they rely on a great cosmic toting up of scores. And if that's the way it works, maybe my dues were paid by those women who were here ahead of me and some entity declared at my birth, *The women in her line have done enough. They have bought a good life for this one. Let her go in peace.*

The value of a family history, or of any history, is that while we have no desire to repeat it, we do need to know it. Our degree of need ranges from detached curiosity to a deep, primeval longing to reach backward into the deepest recesses of time and memory, where we can relive moments of our own childhood.

Whenever my solitary wandering results in a bout of homesickness, I've learned a trick: focusing hard on memory, I move slowly through my house, room after room. I look out its windows, see the way the afternoon light falls across a table, listen to the wind chimes, watch my dogs napping in their chair. All of this reassures me and I feel better. If I needed to, I could reach even further back, to Mamie's room over the tracks, to the familiar sights and sounds of those who loved me and kept me safe, from the beginning of my time here.

And then there's the ring.

For me, the grandma ring is the legacy of four generations of women who made their journeys ahead of me, and it has become, over the years, a kind of personal talisman. It holds strength and courage, humor and love, for these were the gifts of my ancestors. On those few occasions when I've been in deep trouble, or when someone I loved was in great danger, I've found myself almost unconsciously twisting the ring, rubbing it as I might rub a strand of worry beads if Magdalena Weaver had been born in some Mediterranean country instead of a village in Northern Europe.

This much I've learned. Nobody travels alone. These lives we lead are not our own carefully deliberate journeys, but the sum of all the paths traveled by those who were here before us, one upon the other, step by step, layer upon layer. Life upon life.

There's a stone on Pearl's hill now, one smooth oval of Cenozoic rock my brother found in the summer of 1996 on the old homestead, near the foundation where Mamie's dream house used to stand. It's a piece of prehistory, this rock, one of the rounded, flattish stones that belong to the backbone of the southern prairies, that broken ridge of the Missouri Coteau, which starts where the Cypress Hills move southeast to become Old Man On His Back Plateau and Pinto Butte and Sevenmile Butte and the Killdeer badlands and then Wood Mountain just before they head into Montana. Rocks like these tumbled downward as the Rocky Mountains pushed upward, and when by the continual grinding of plate against plate other rock beds turned to rivers of gravel, these high

places of the prairie backbone kept some of the stones for themselves, before tumbling them into a stream, which rounded and
smoothed them. Such stones have a peculiar beauty, their shape and
color being not unlike a loaf of freeform bread baked in a wood-
fired oven.

This one looks useful and invites touching.

My brother had it engraved: *Pearl Godin, 1918–1990.*

It's not a big stone, so the rest of the inscription is only in my
mind: *She was Mamie's daughter.* Here on Pearl's hill, it's easy to feel my
family of amiable ghosts all around me.

Magdalena, with her thick Bavarian accent, looking at me
through narrowed eyes, *This one is taller than the rest of us.*

Sophia, speaking softly, *Is that my ring she's wearing?*

Mamie, in a pleased voice, *It's real pretty up here. I like the view.*

Pearl, looking at me, *Really, child. When are you going to do something
with your hair?*

We'd have so much to talk about now that they've all moved on
and the world must be going finally and irretrievably to the dogs.

Bibliography

Brunsdon, Myrtle. Personal interview. 1997.

Carter, Sarah. *Lost Harvests: Prairie Reserve Farmers and Government Policy.* Montreal: McGill–Queen's University Press, 1990.

De Brou, David. *Other Voices: Historical Essays on Saskatchewan Women.* Regina: Canadian Plains Research Centre, University of Regina, 1995.

Dodge, David. "The Meaning of May 10" and "Can We Save the Native Prairie?" *Borealis* Fall 1989.

Friesen, Gerald. *The Canadian Prairies: A History.* Toronto: University of Toronto Press, 1984.

Gayton, Don. *The Wheatgrass Mechanism: Science and Imagination in the Western Canadian Landscape.* Saskatoon: Fifth House, 1990.

Handlin, Oscar. *The Uprooted.* Toronto: Little, Brown, 1979.

Harris, Kenneth. Personal interviews. 1996, 1997.

Harris, Roland. Taped interview. 1975

Harris, Roland. Private papers. 1980.

Harris, Violet. Personal interviews. 1997.

Heat-Moon, William Least. *Prairyerth*. Boston: Houghton Mifflin, 1991.

Love, Myron. "The Red River Tall Grass Prairie Revival." *Borealis*. Fall 1991.

Poirier, Thelma. *Grasslands*. Regina: Coteau Books, 1990.

Potyondi, Barry. *In Palliser's Triangle: Living in the Grasslands, 1850–1930*. Saskatoon: Purich Publishing, 1995.

Schlissel, Lillian. *Women's Diaries of the Westward Journey*. New York: Schocken Books, 1982.

Spry, Irene M. *The Palliser Expedition: An Account of John Palliser's British North American Exploring Expedition, 1857–1860*. Saskatoon: Fifth House, 1995.

Stegner, Wallace. *Wolf Willow: A History, A Story, and A Memory of the Last Plains Frontier*. Toronto: Macmillan of Canada, 1955.

Storrie, Kathleen. *Women, Isolation and Bonding: The Ecology of Gender*. Toronto: Methuen Publications, 1987.

Wood Mountain Historical Society. *They Came to Wood Mountain*. Wood Mountain: Wood Mountain Historical Society, 1967.